I0751981

Always in the Dark

ANNE HOPKINS

For more information about the artist visit http://www.annehopkinsphotography.com
For more information on all RMR Press publications visit our website at:
http://www.rmr-press.com

First Edition

10 9 8 7 6 5 4 3 2 1
Printed in the United States of America

ISBN : 978-0-6151-6675-9

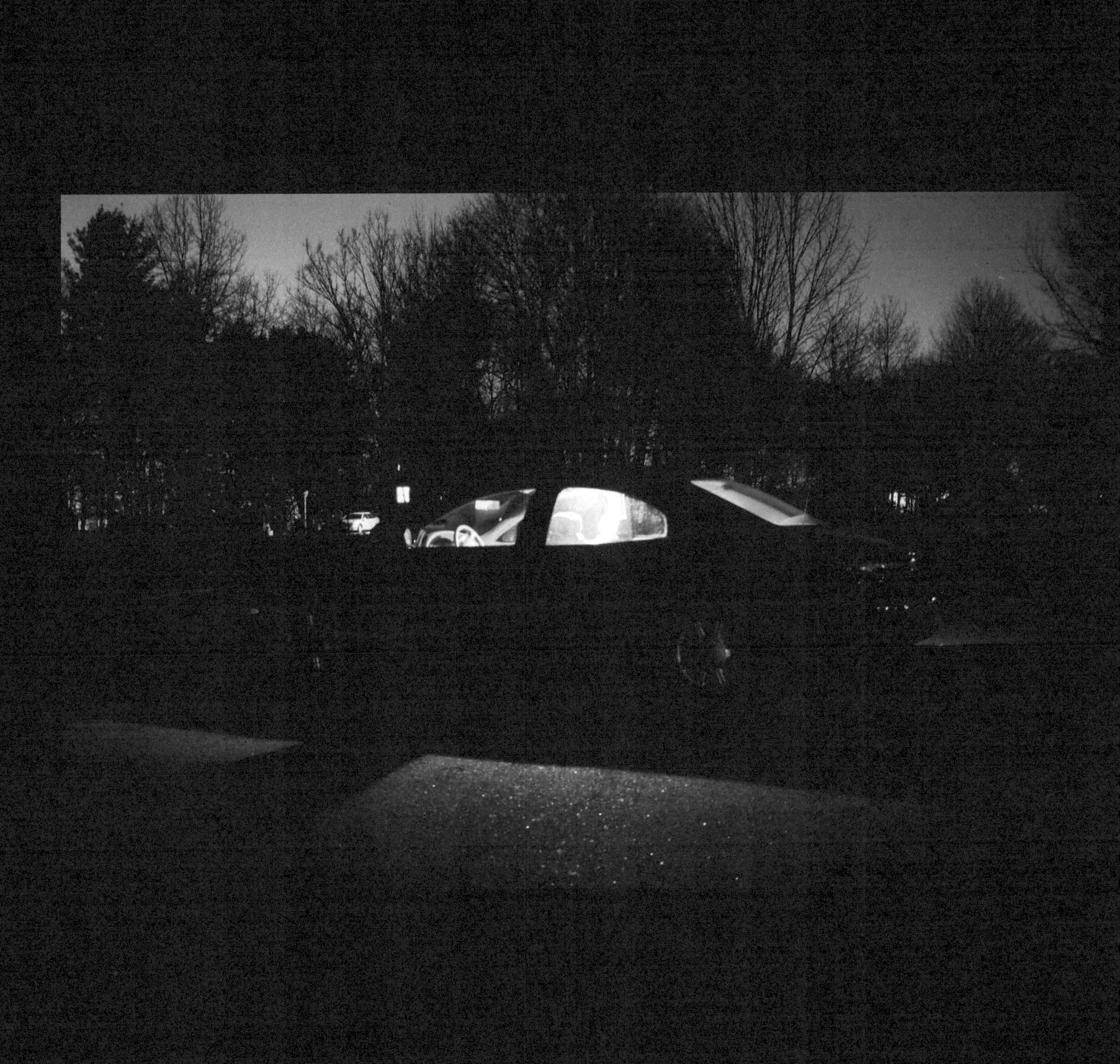

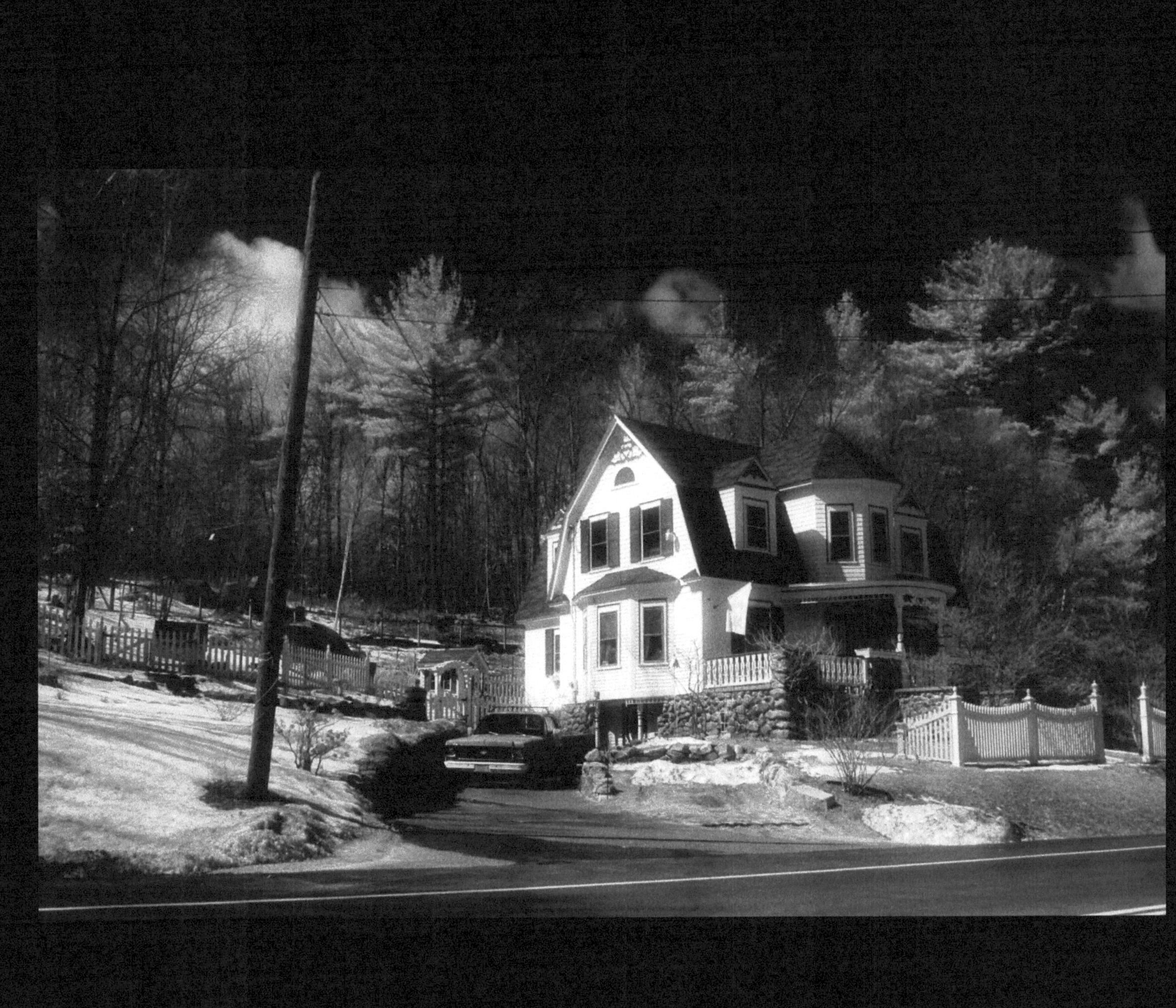

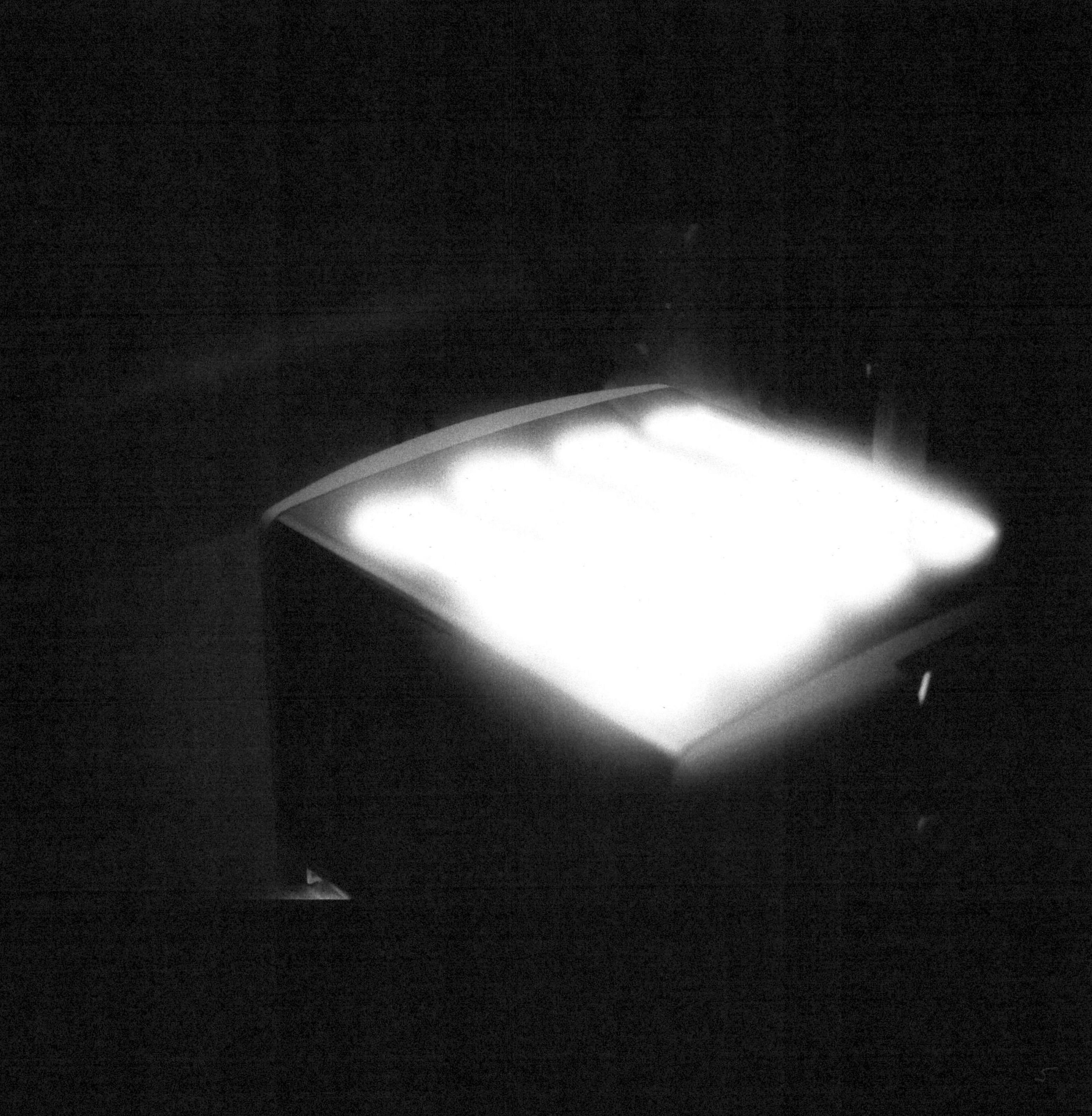

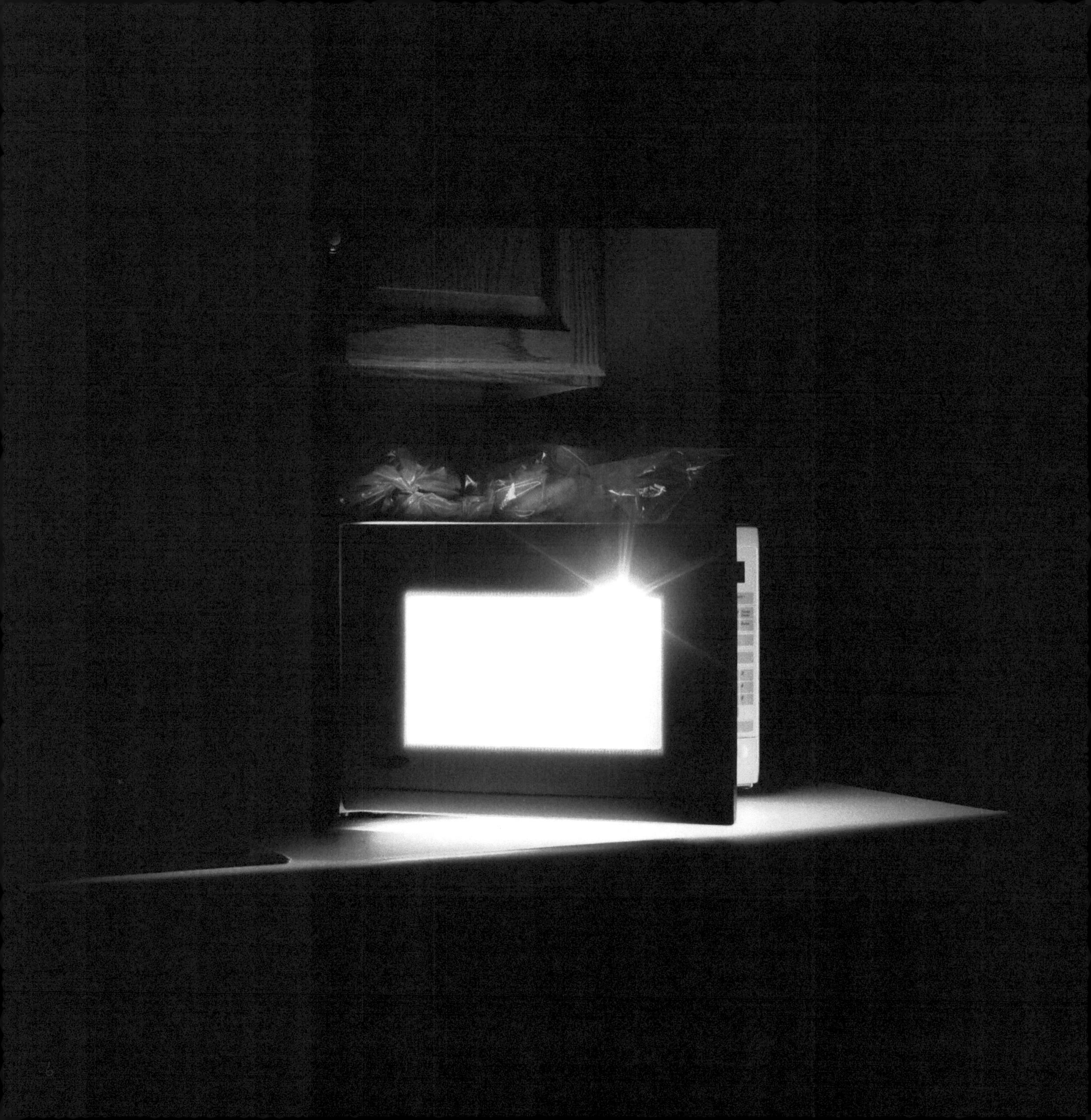

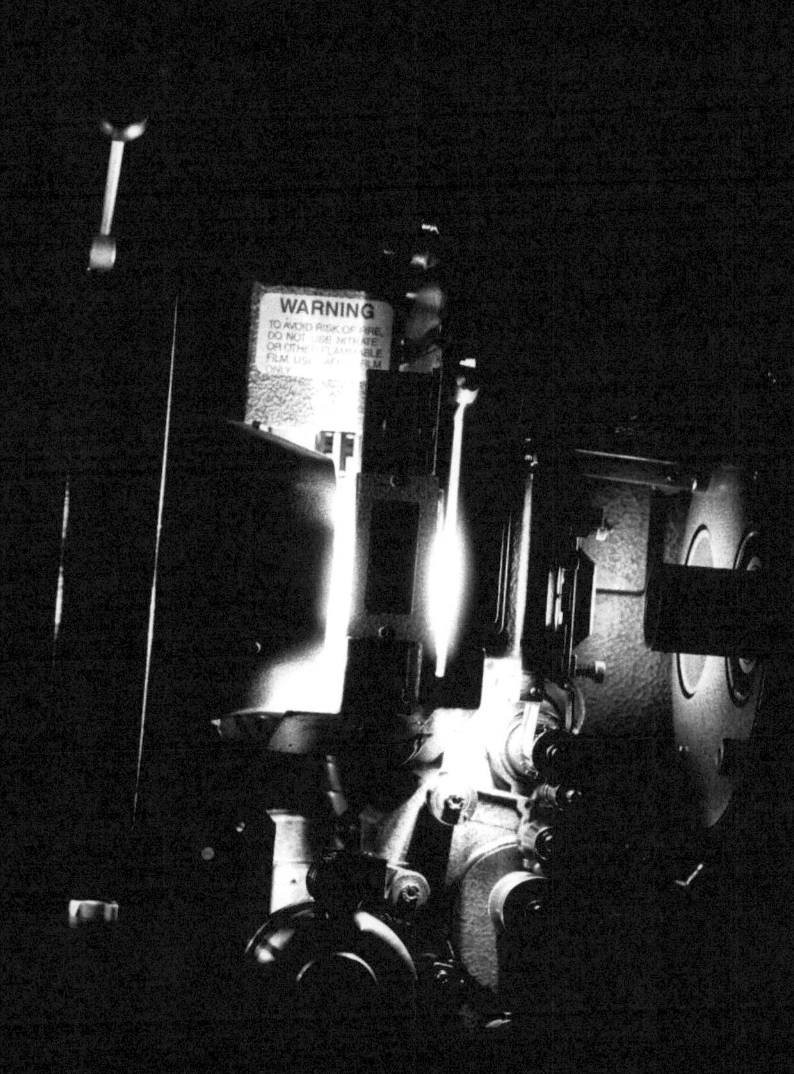
WARNING
TO AVOID RISK OF FIRE,
DO NOT USE NITRATE

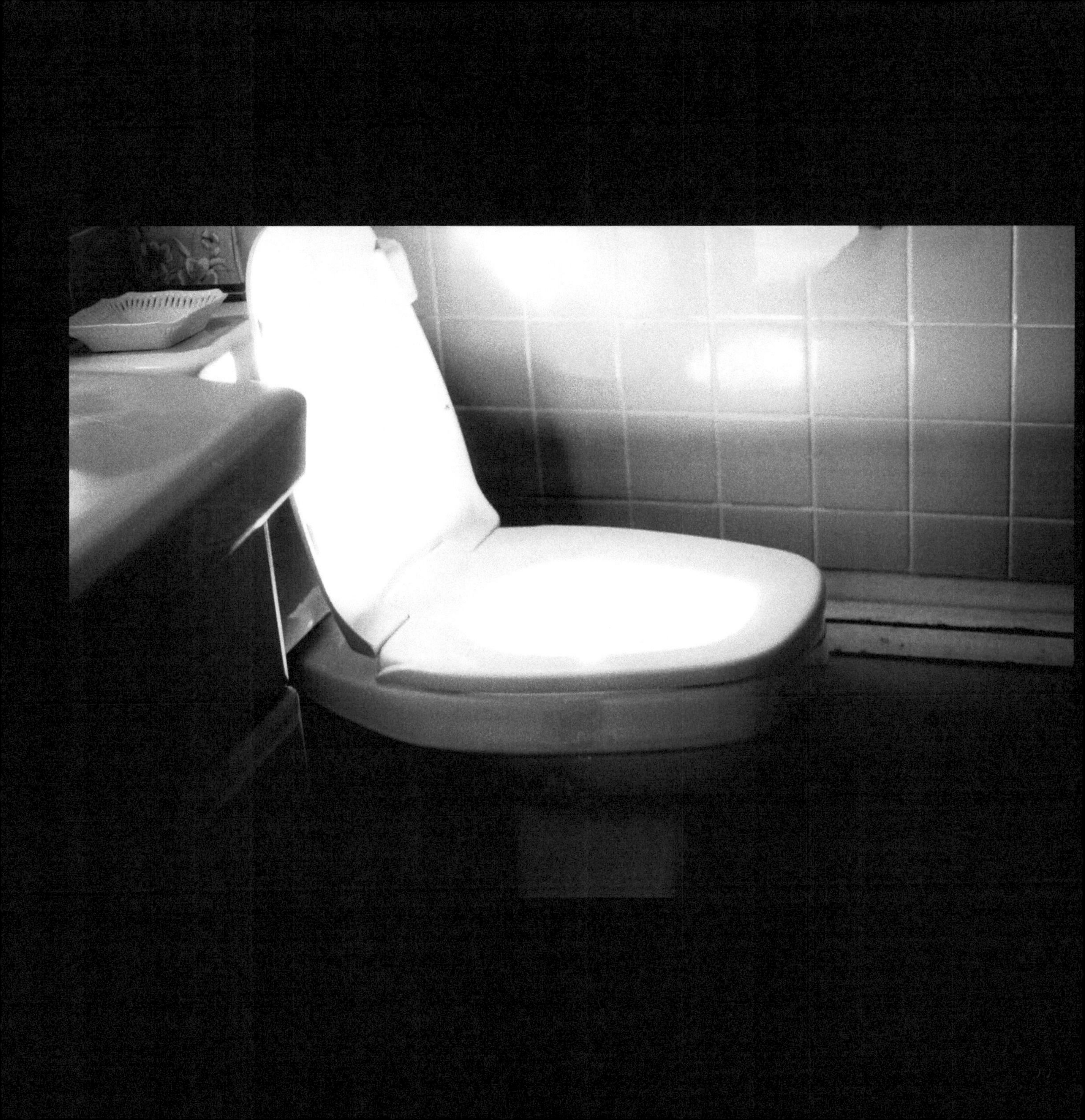

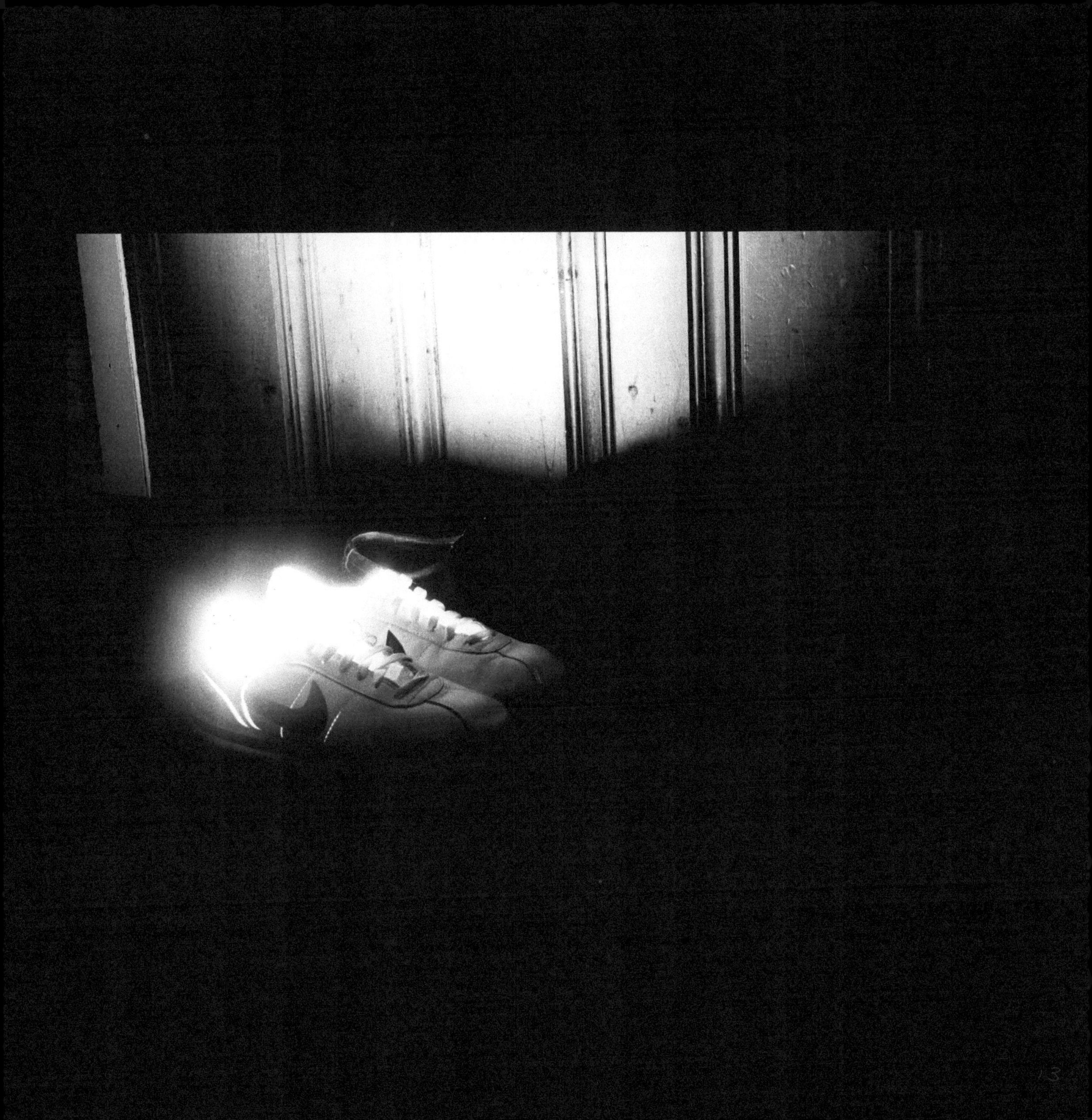

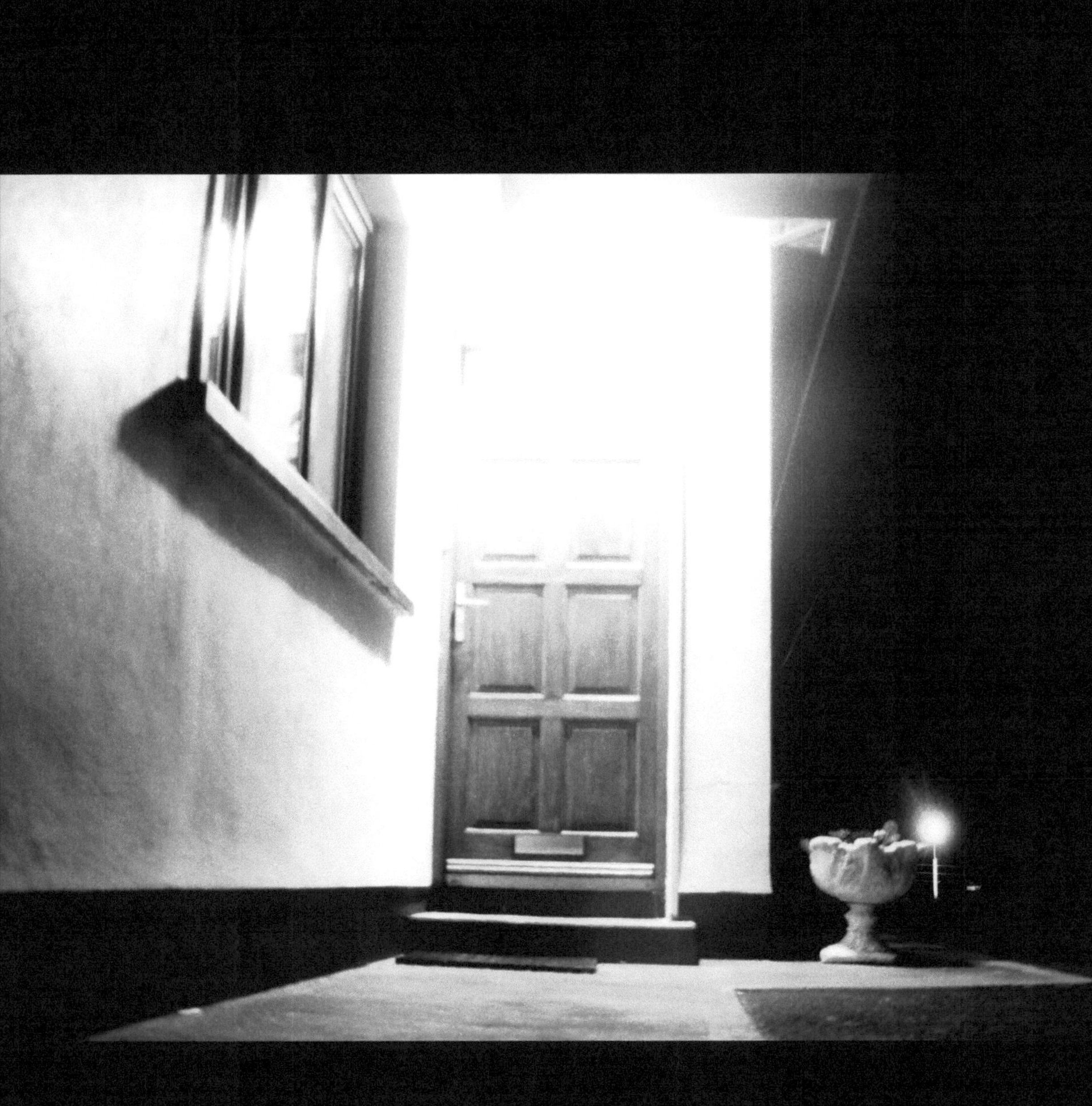

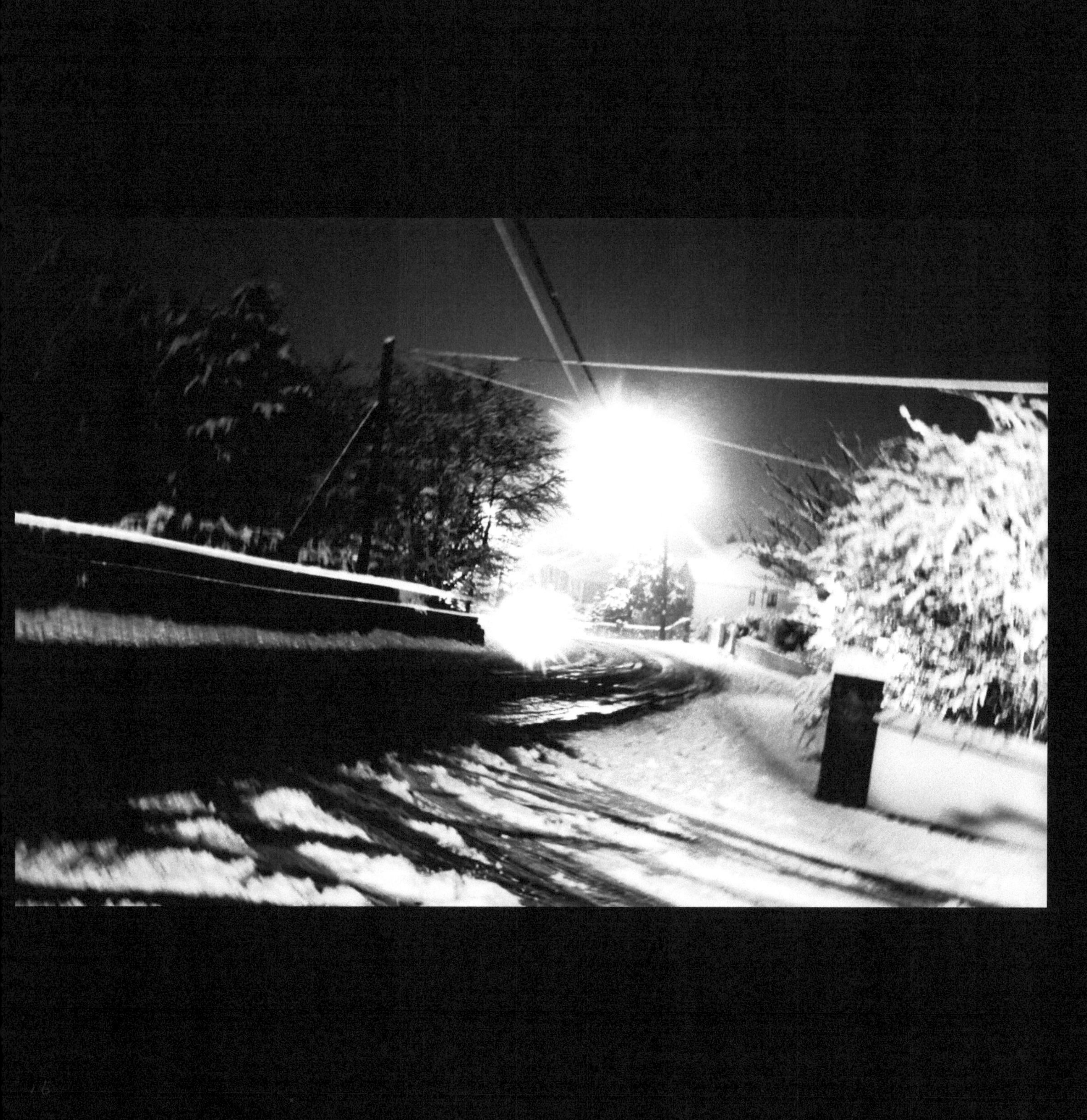

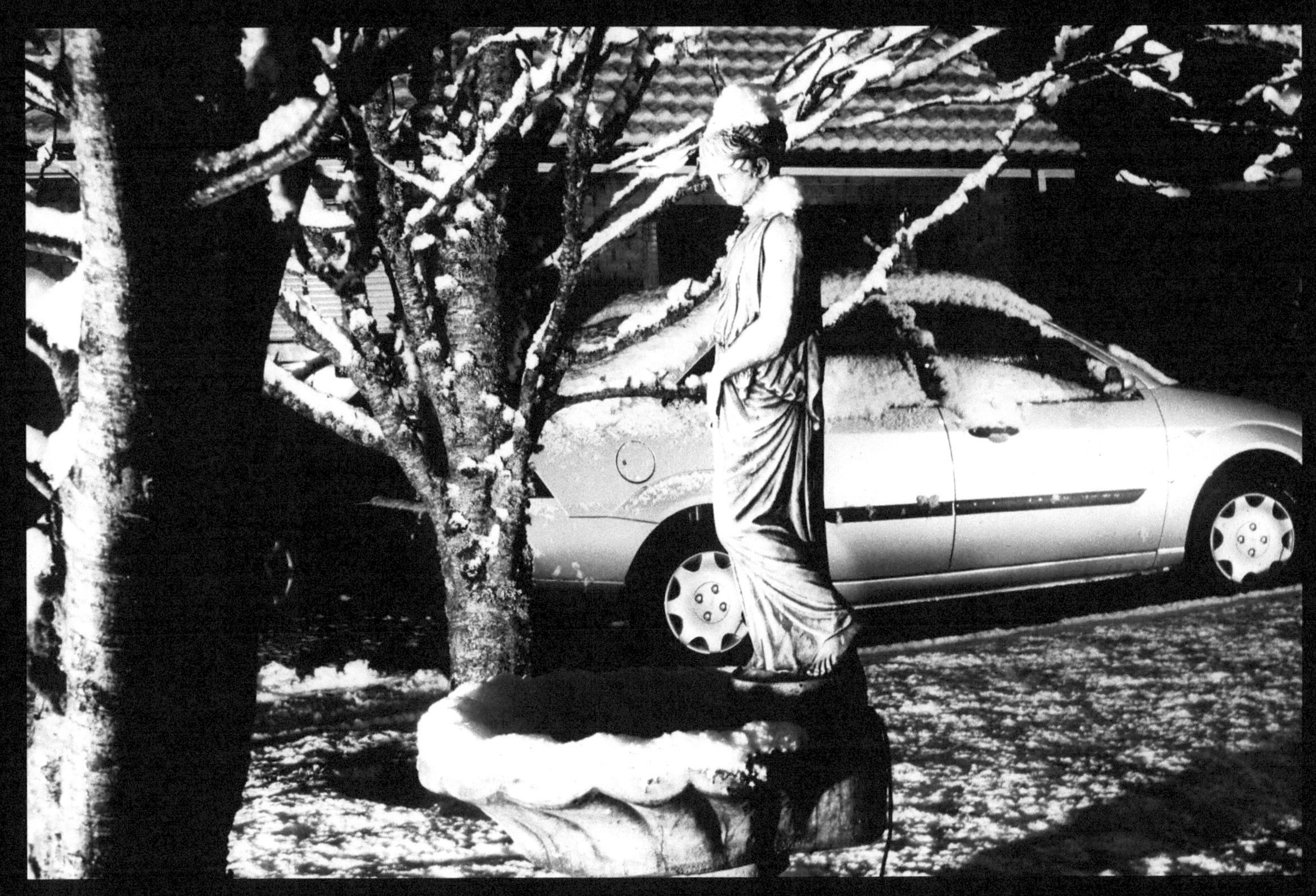

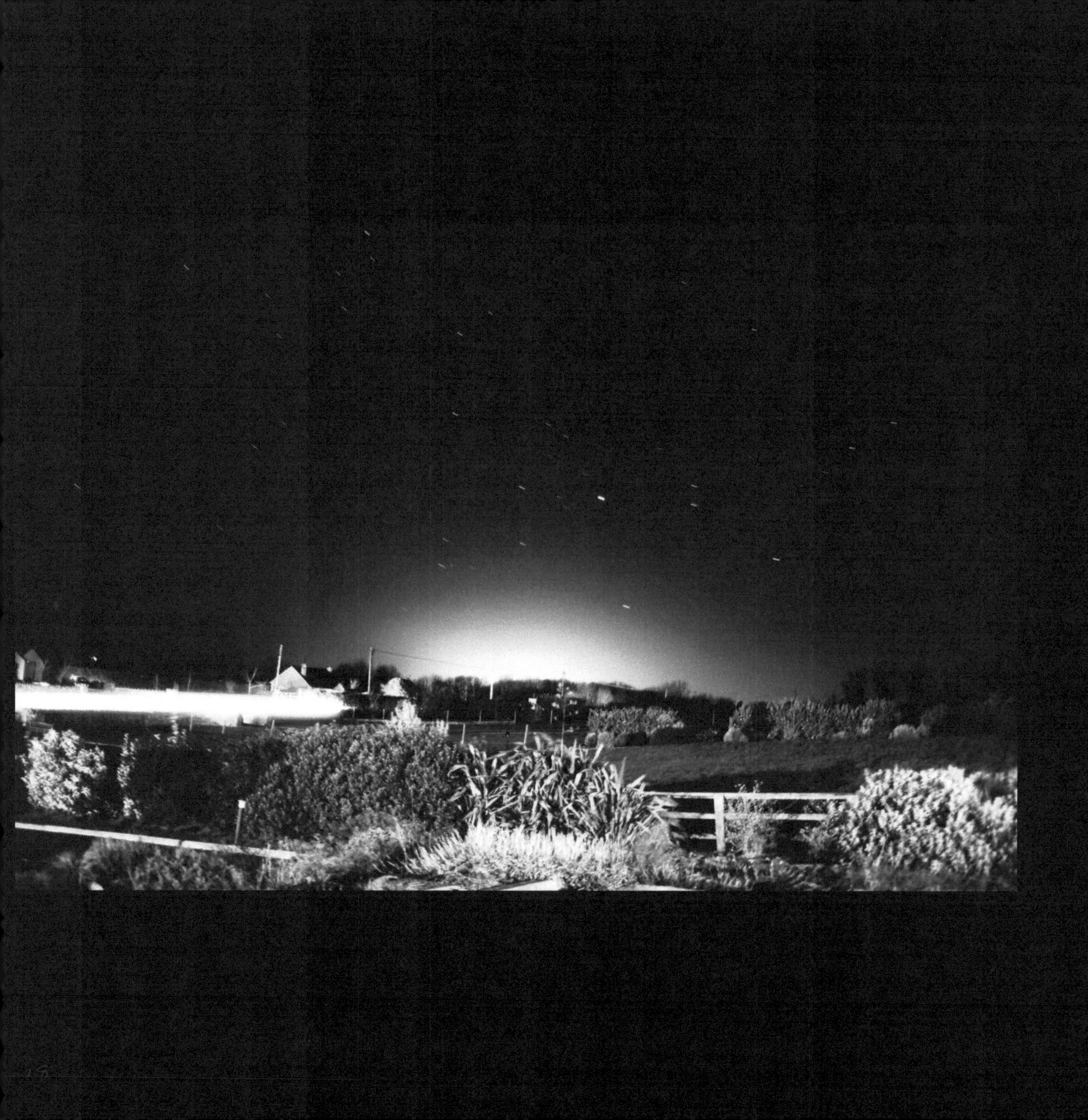

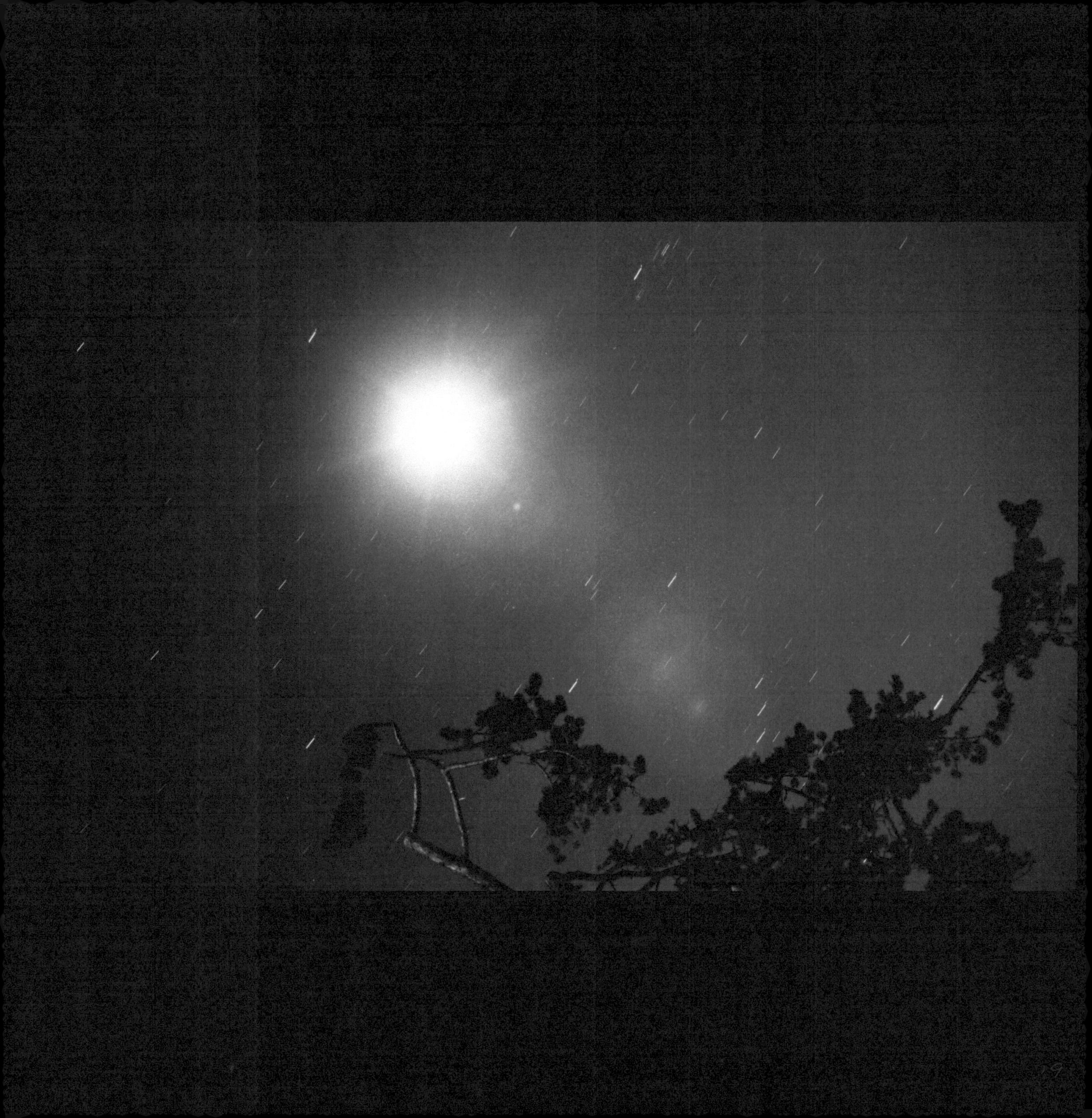

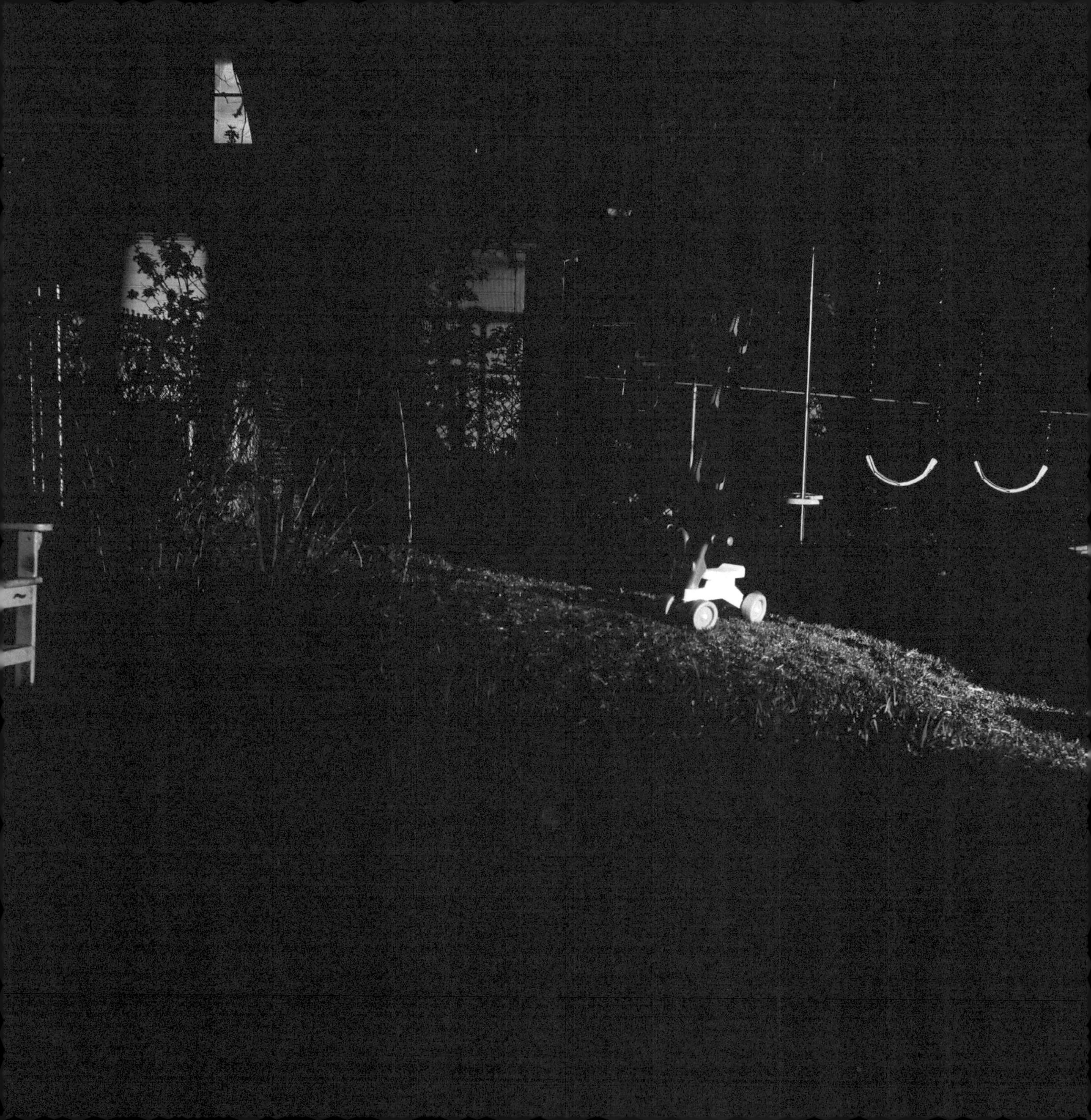

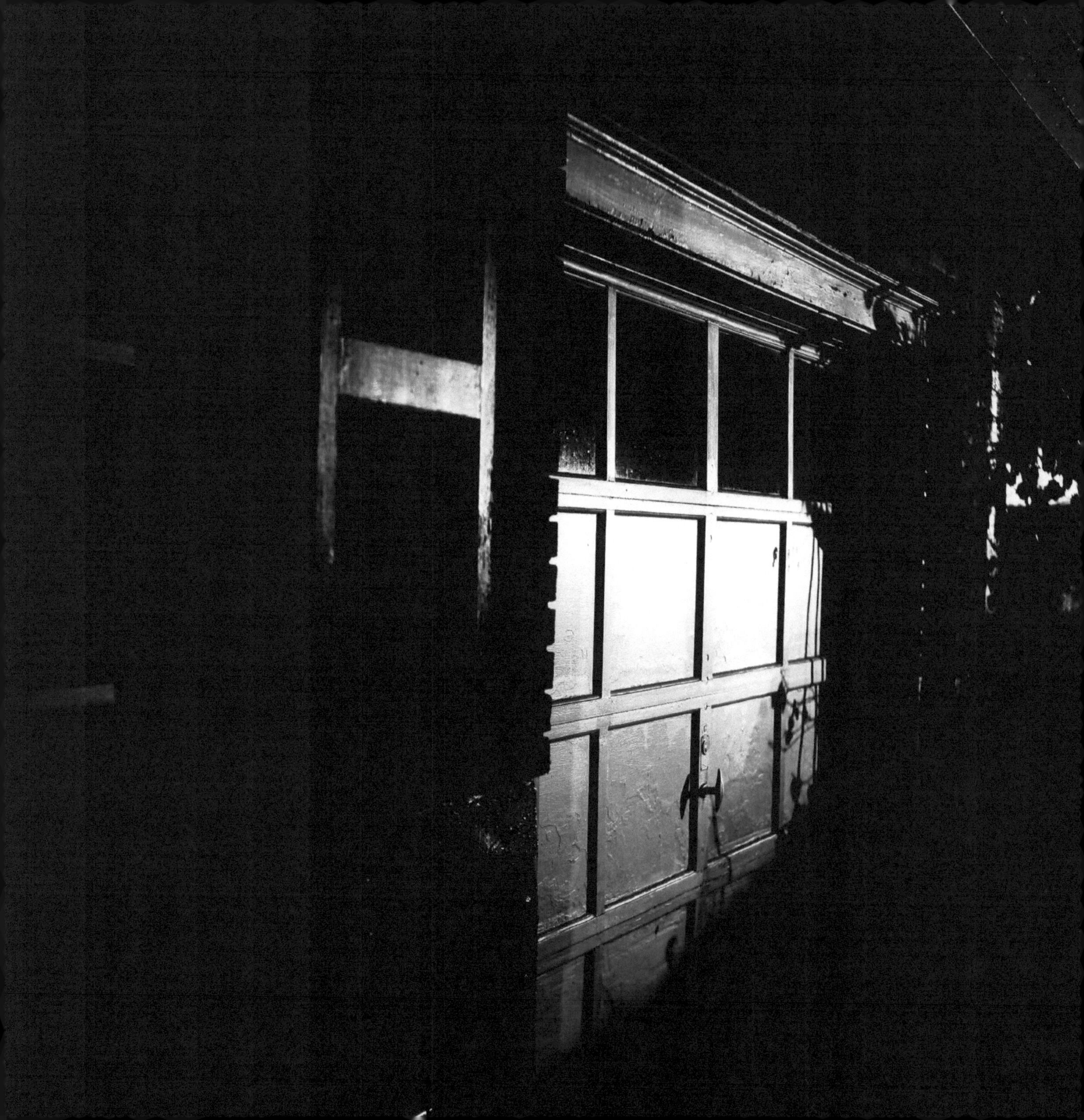

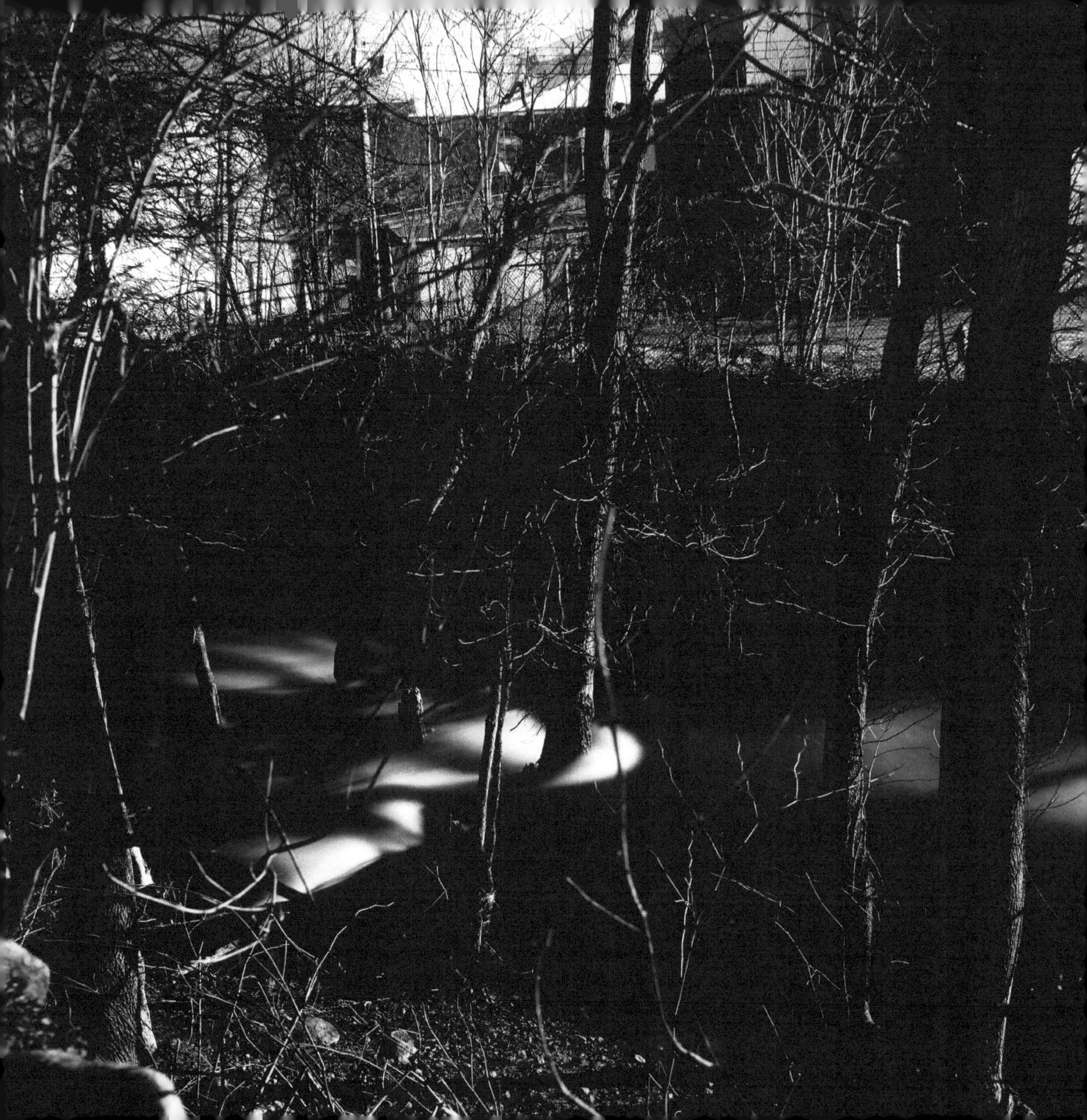

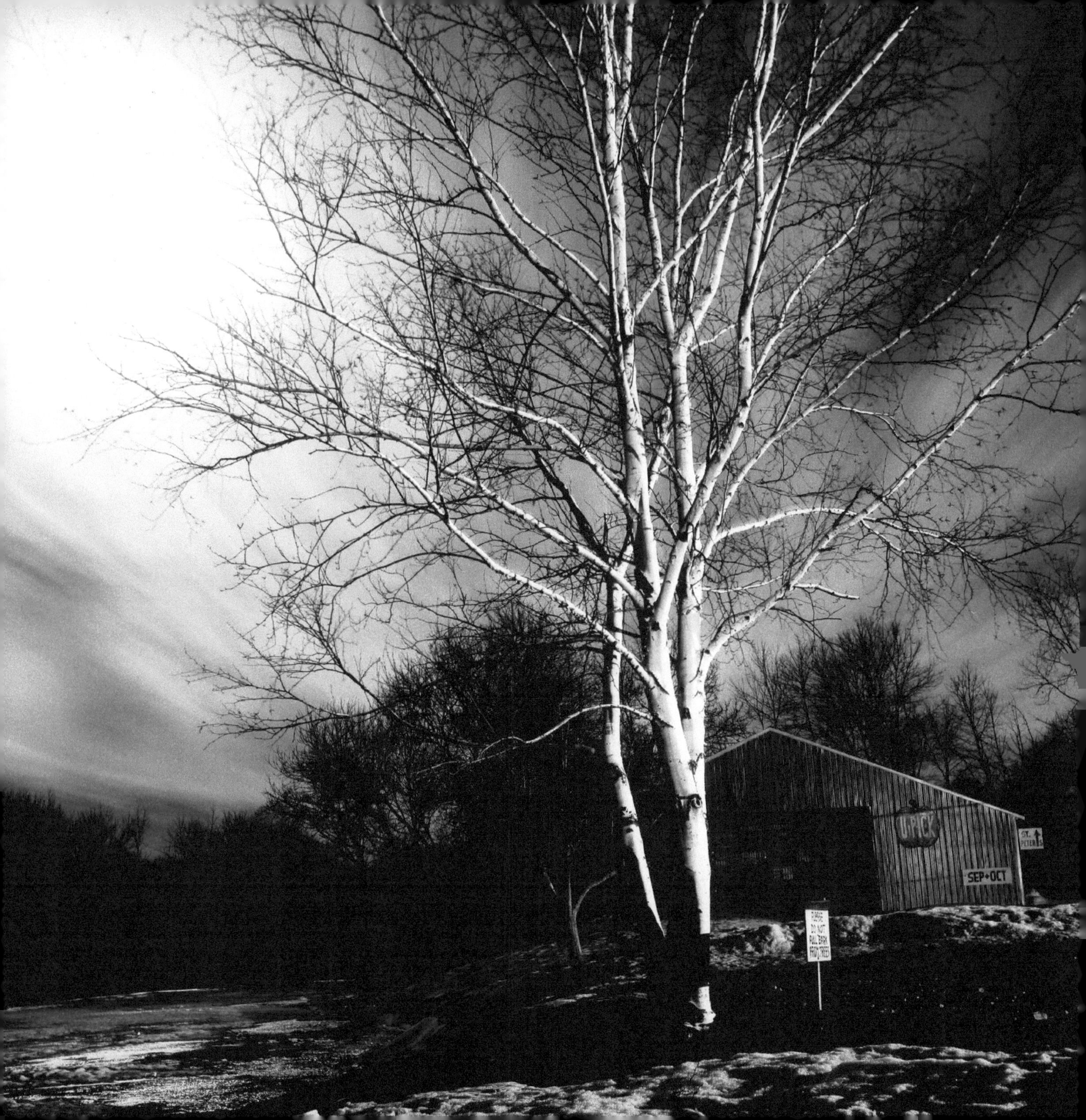
U-PICK
ST. PETERS
SEP + OCT
DO NOT
PULL BARK
FROM TREES

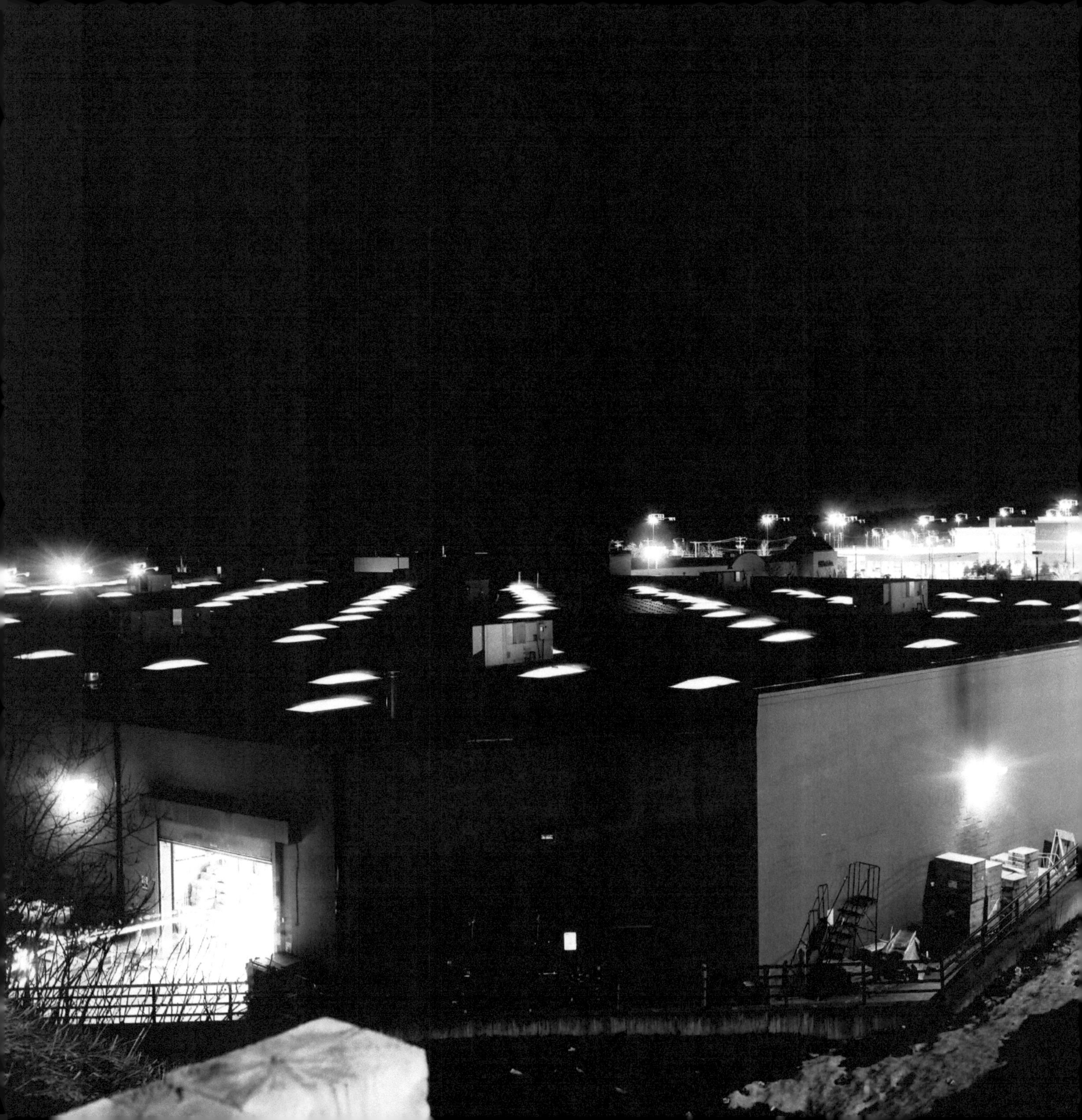

ENGINES
PLUS

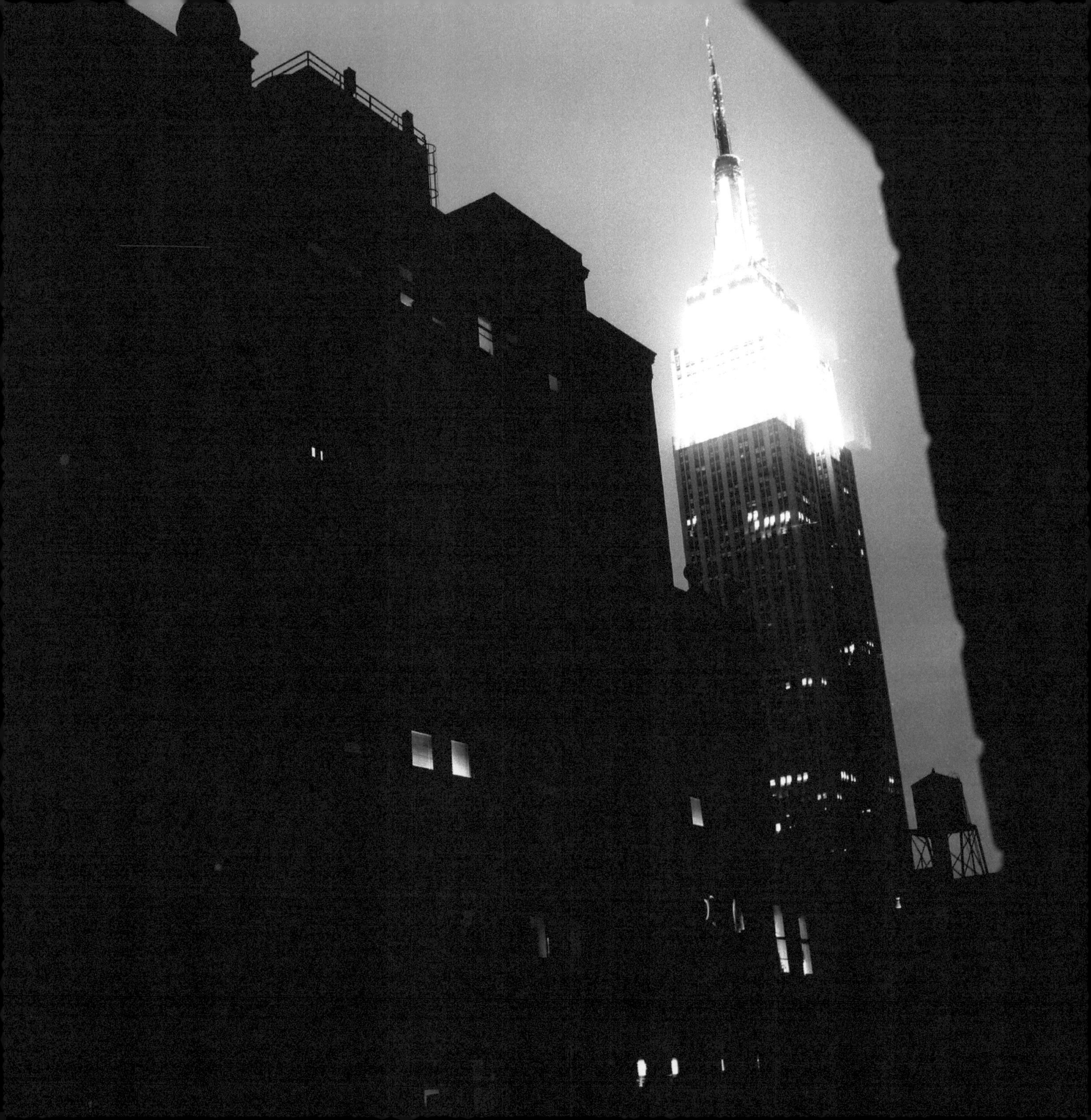

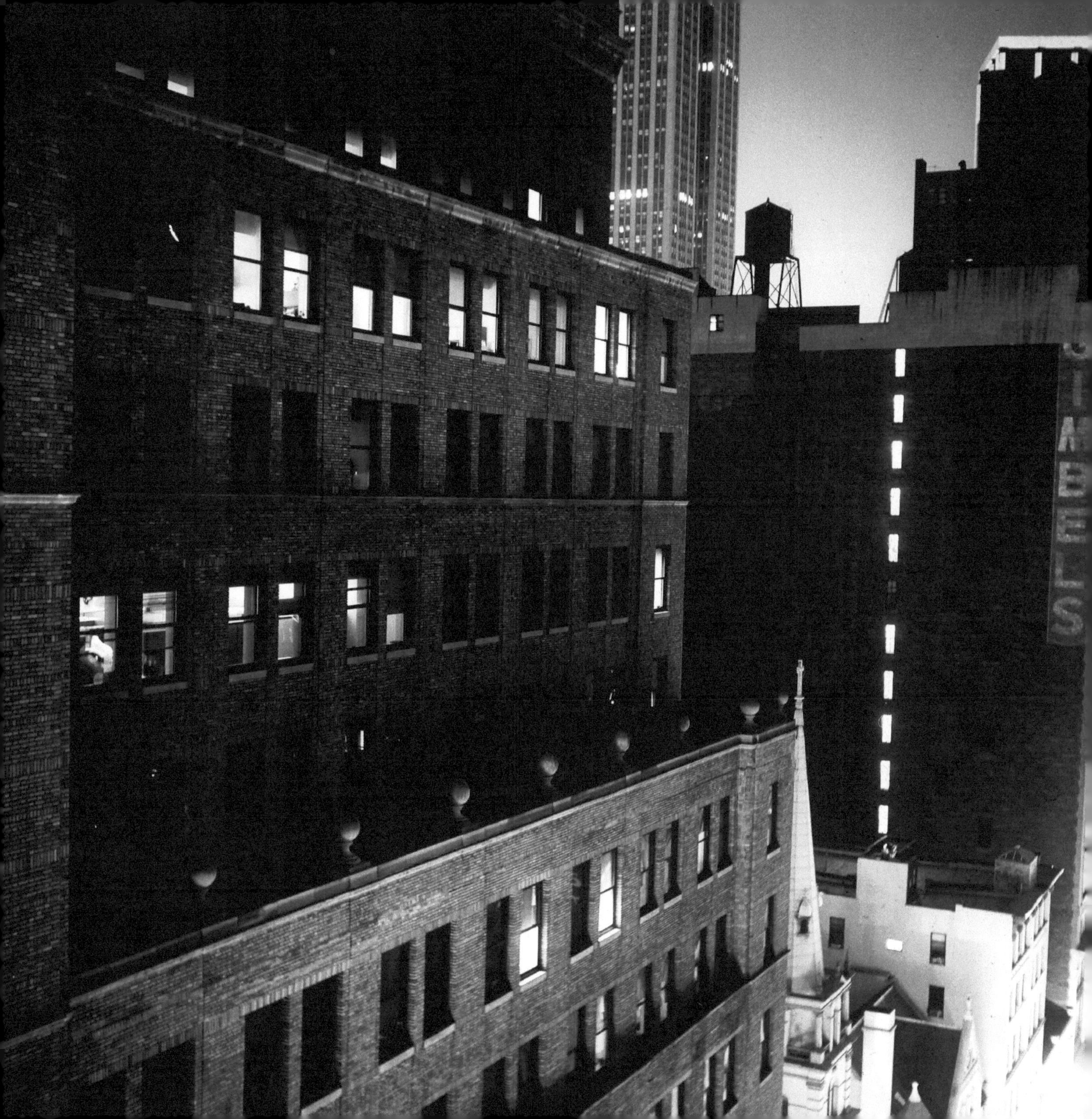

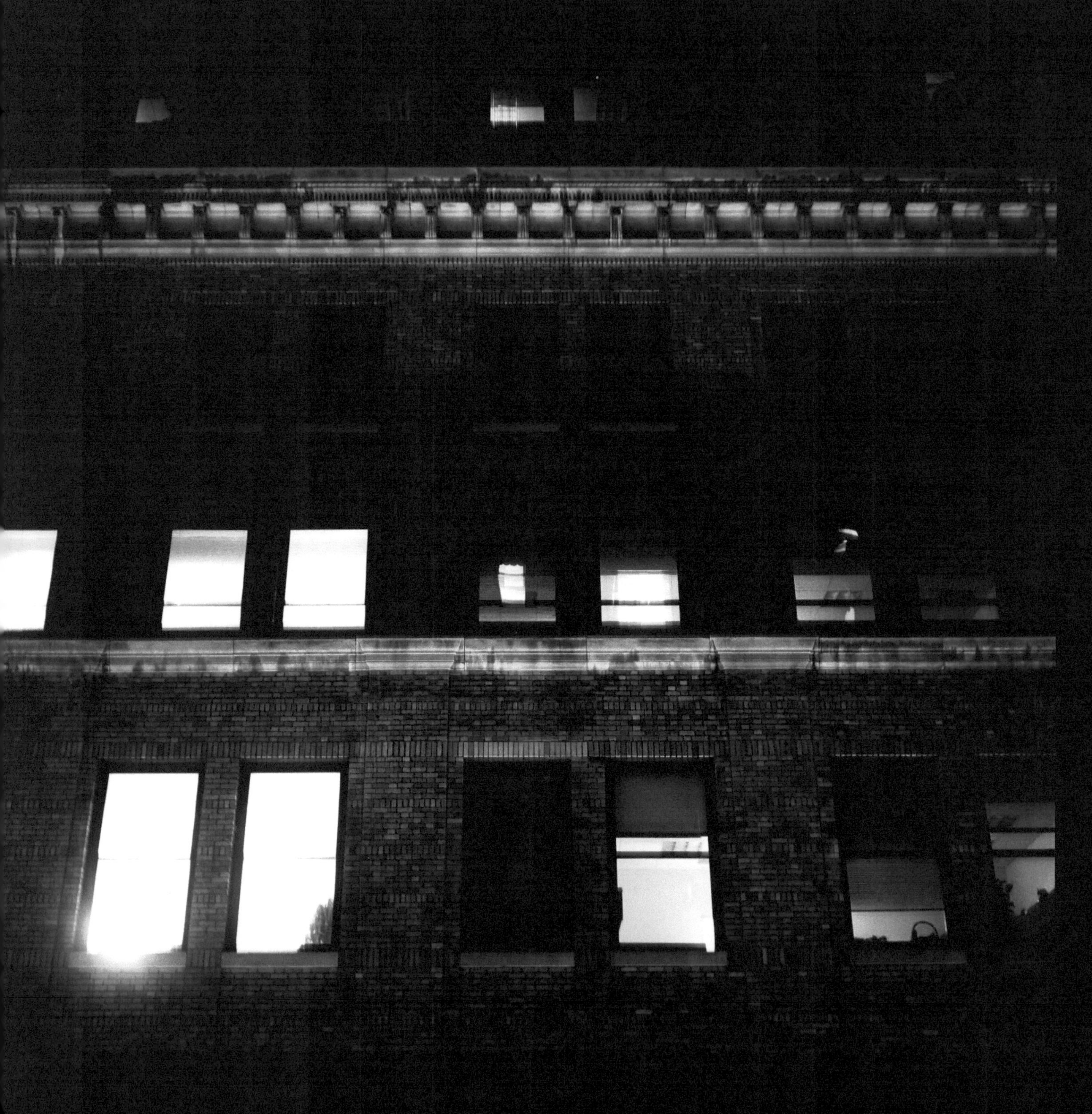

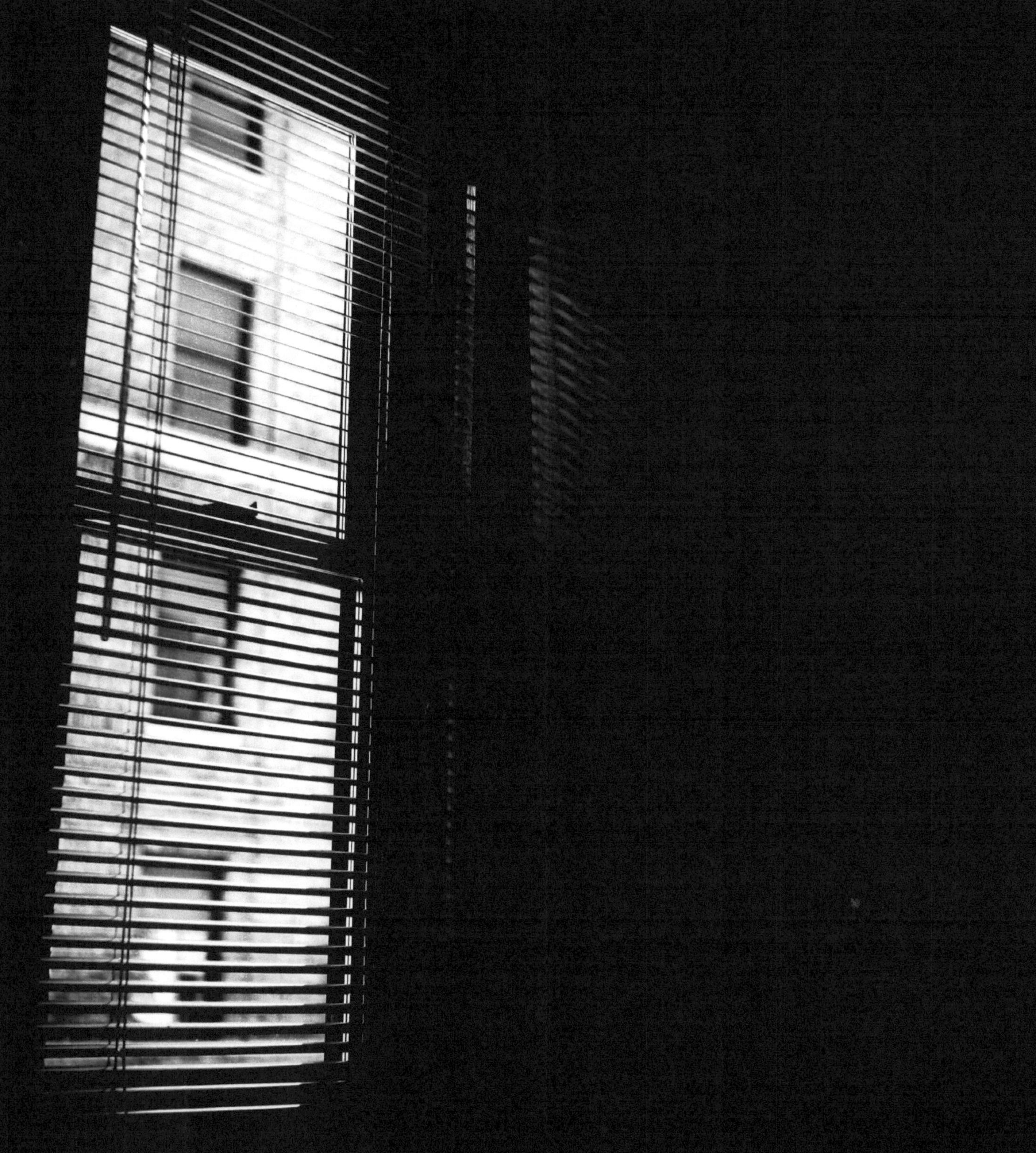

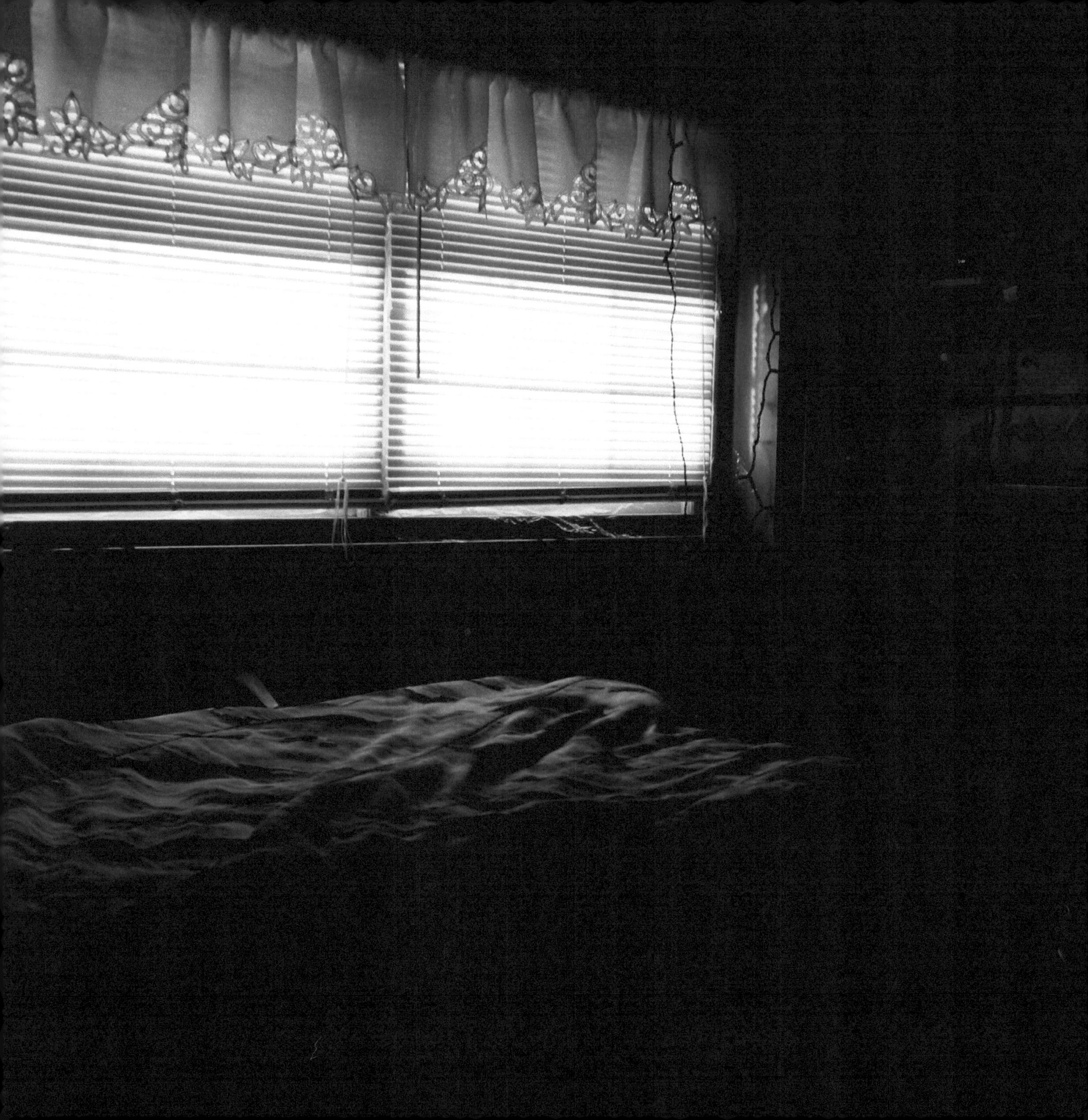

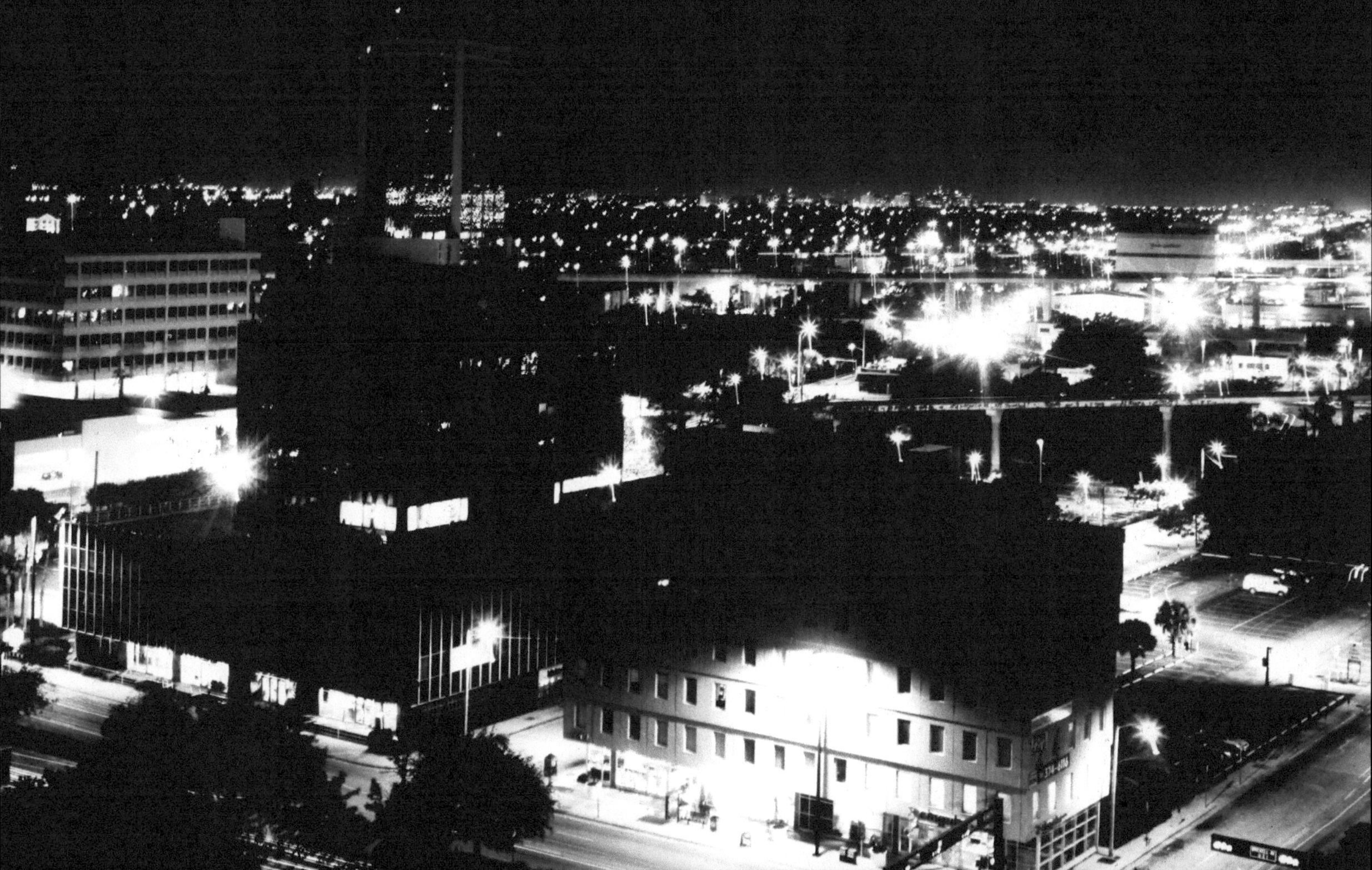

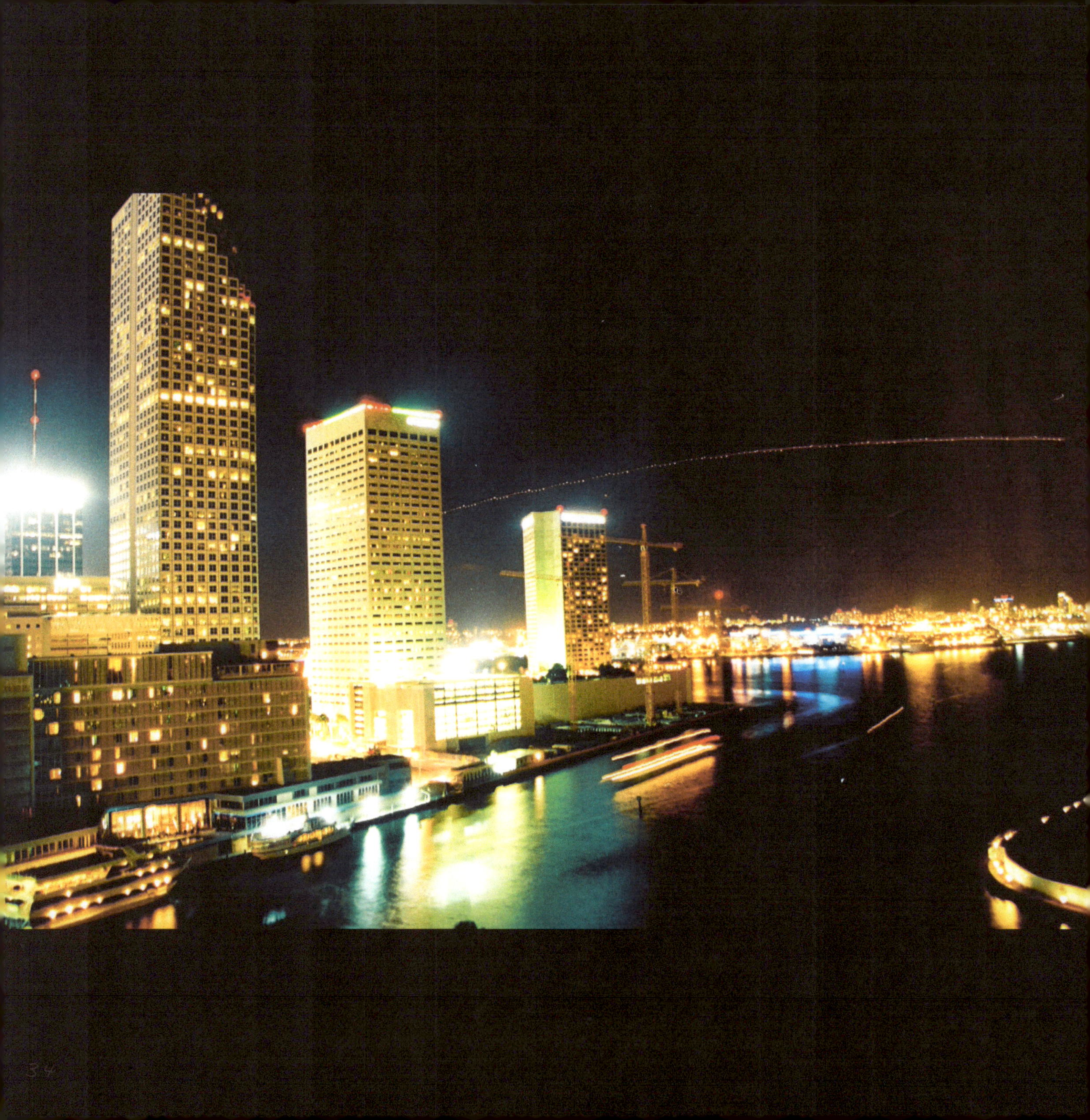

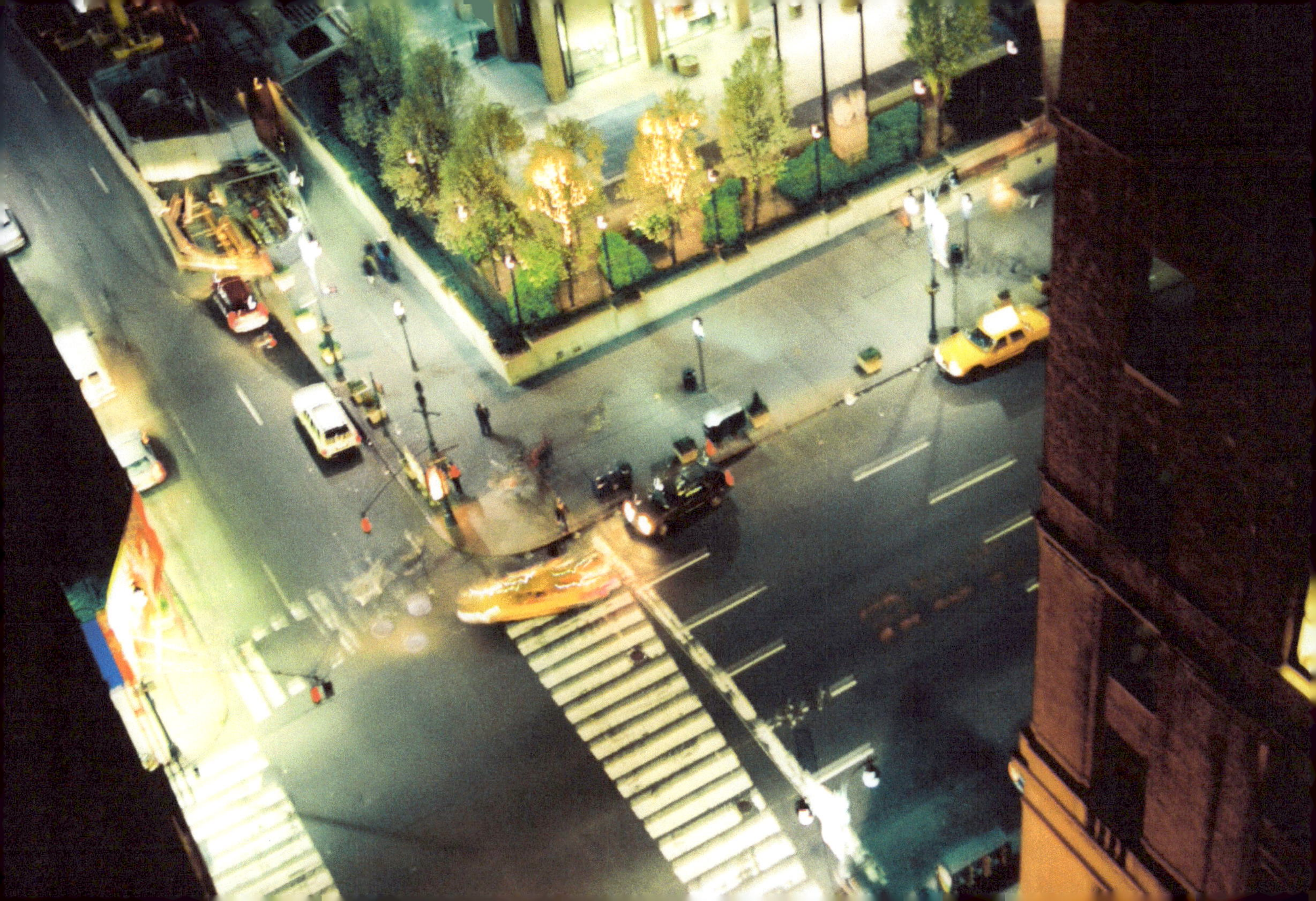

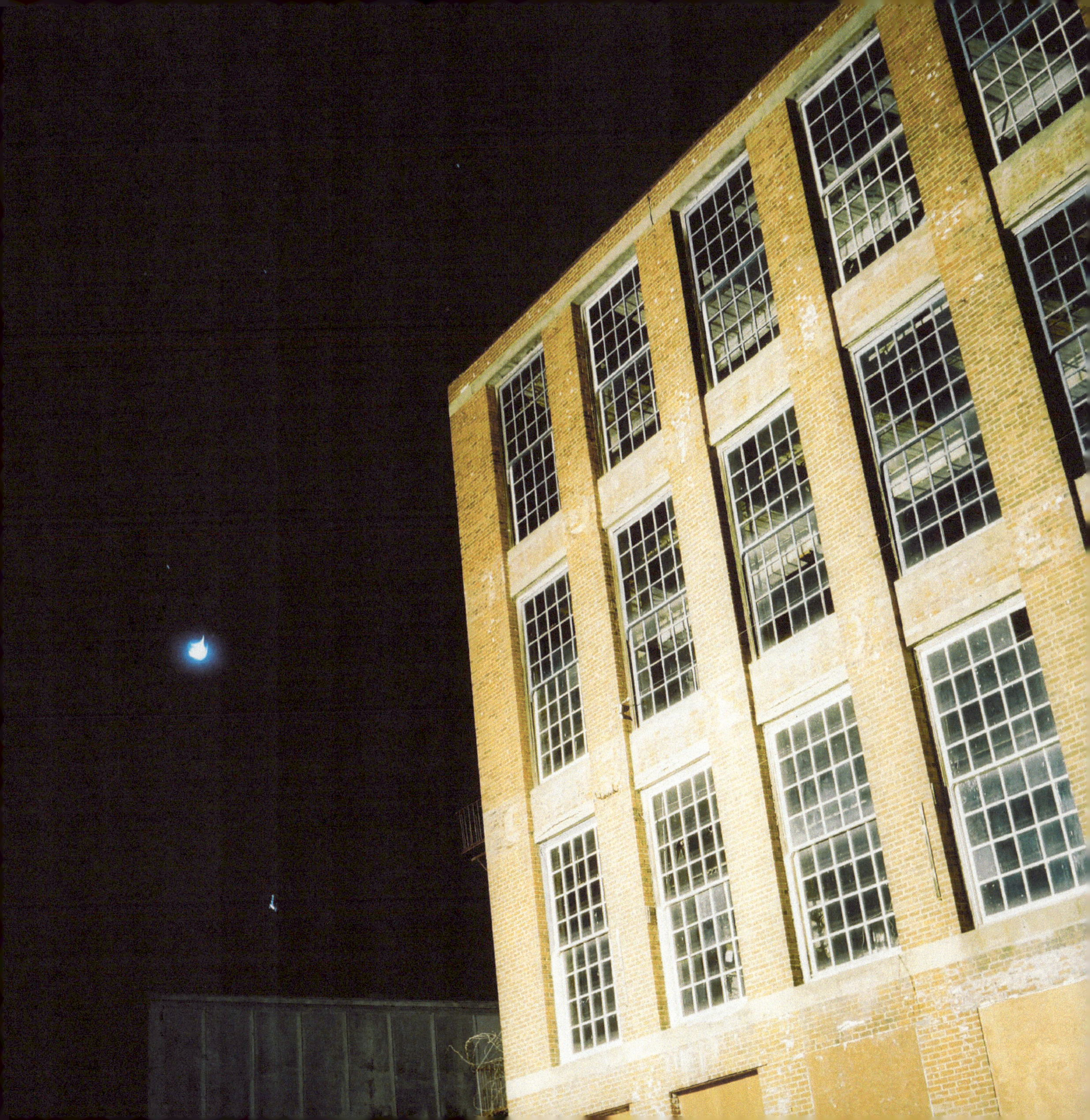

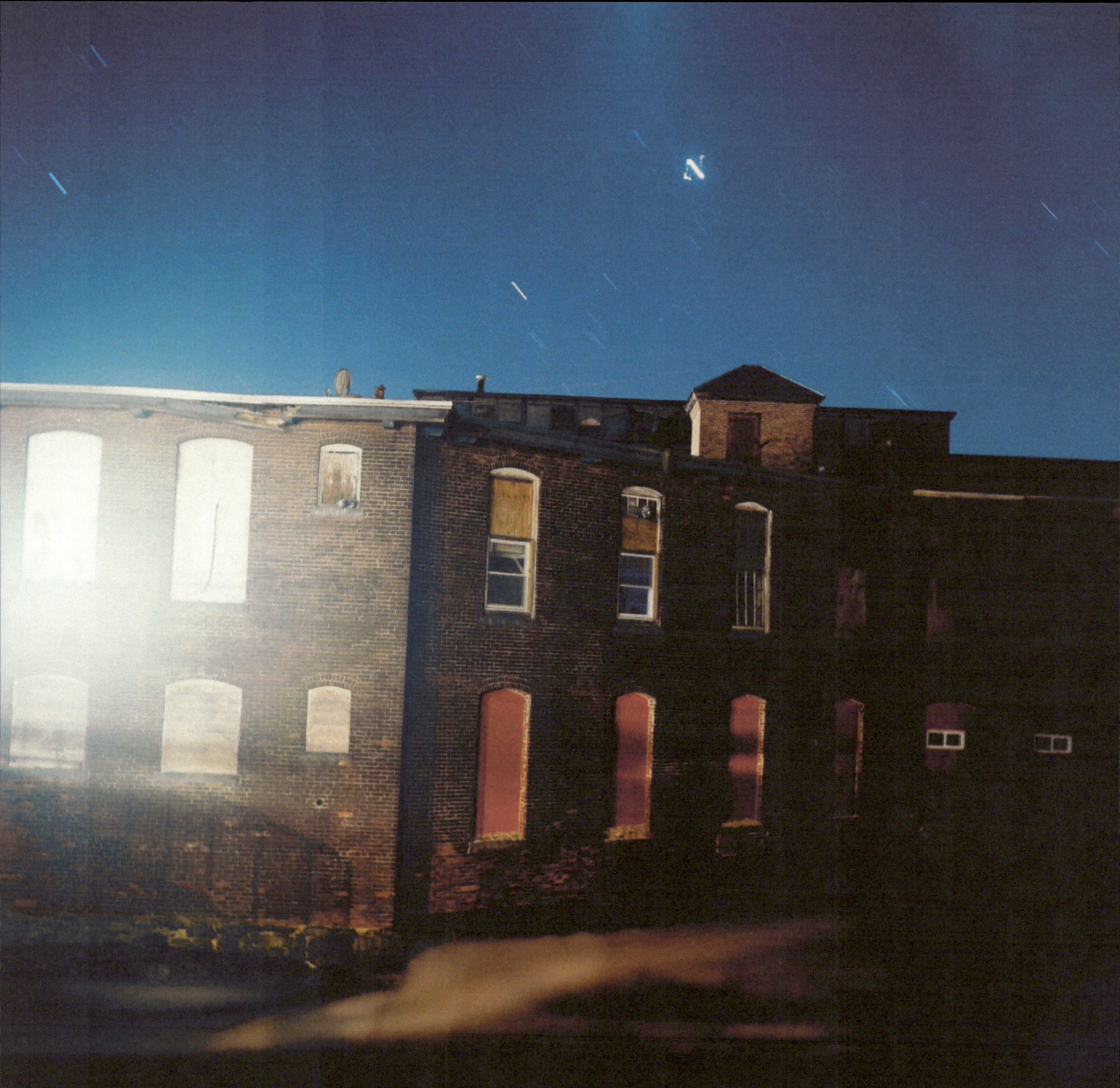

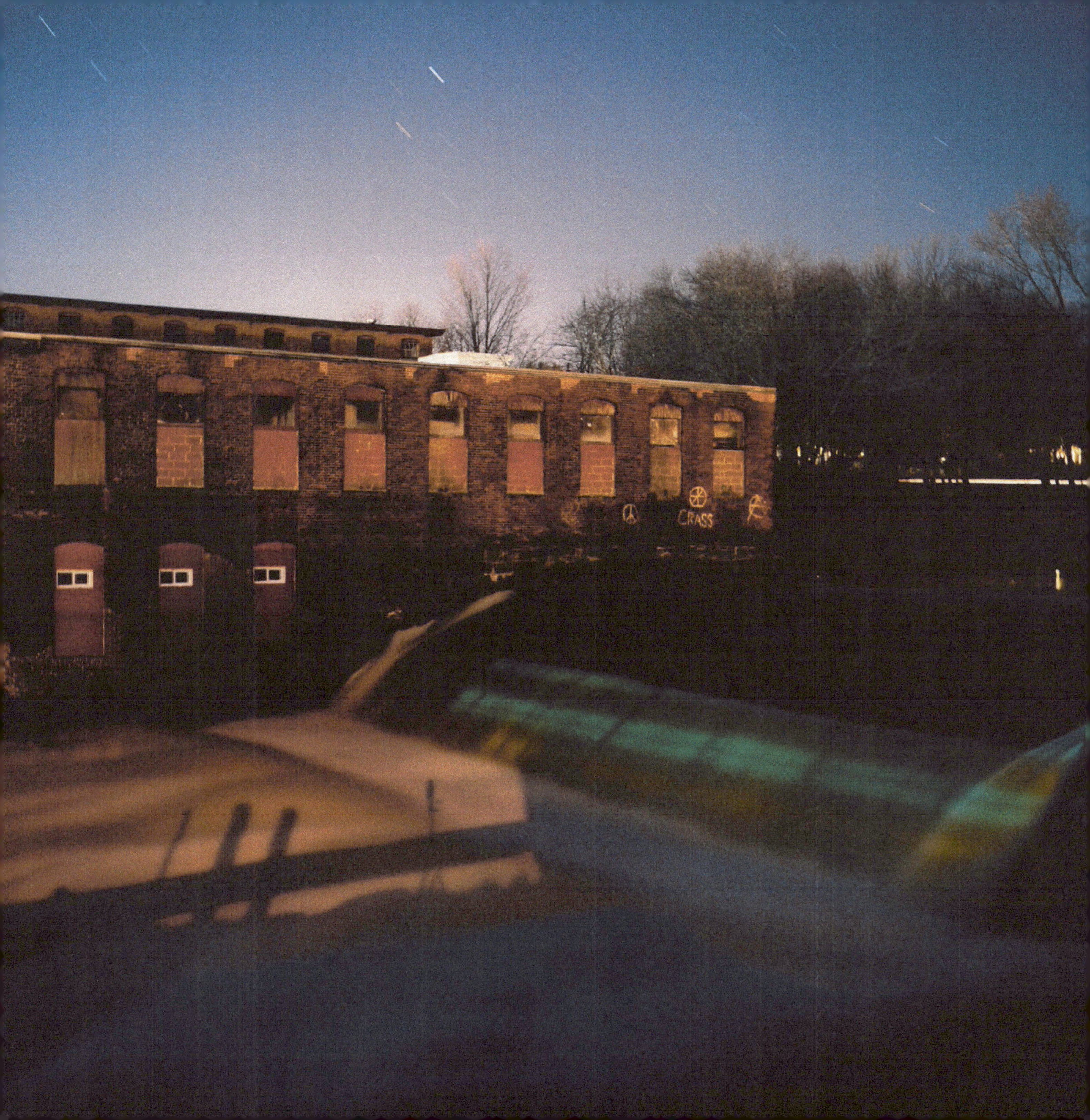
CRASS

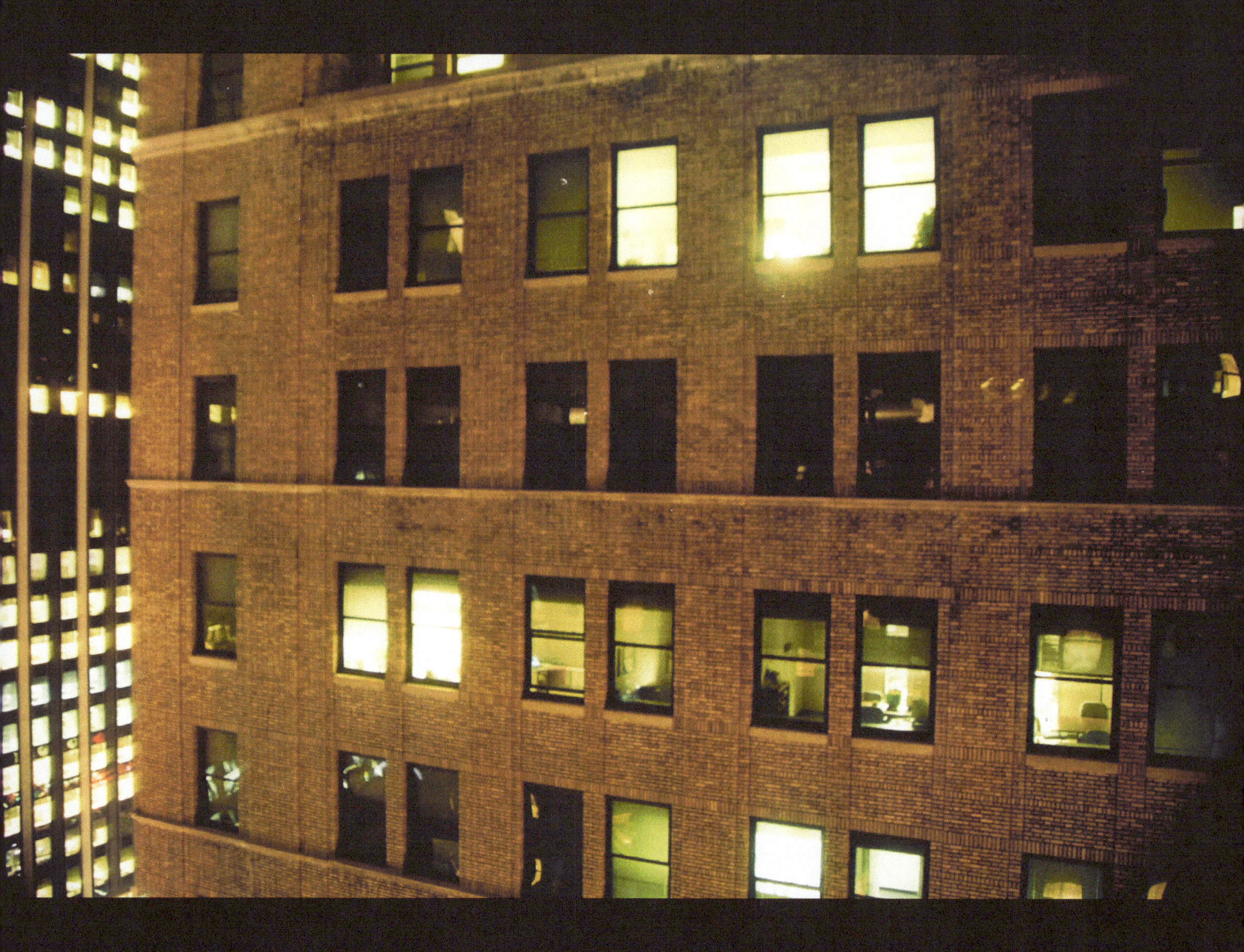

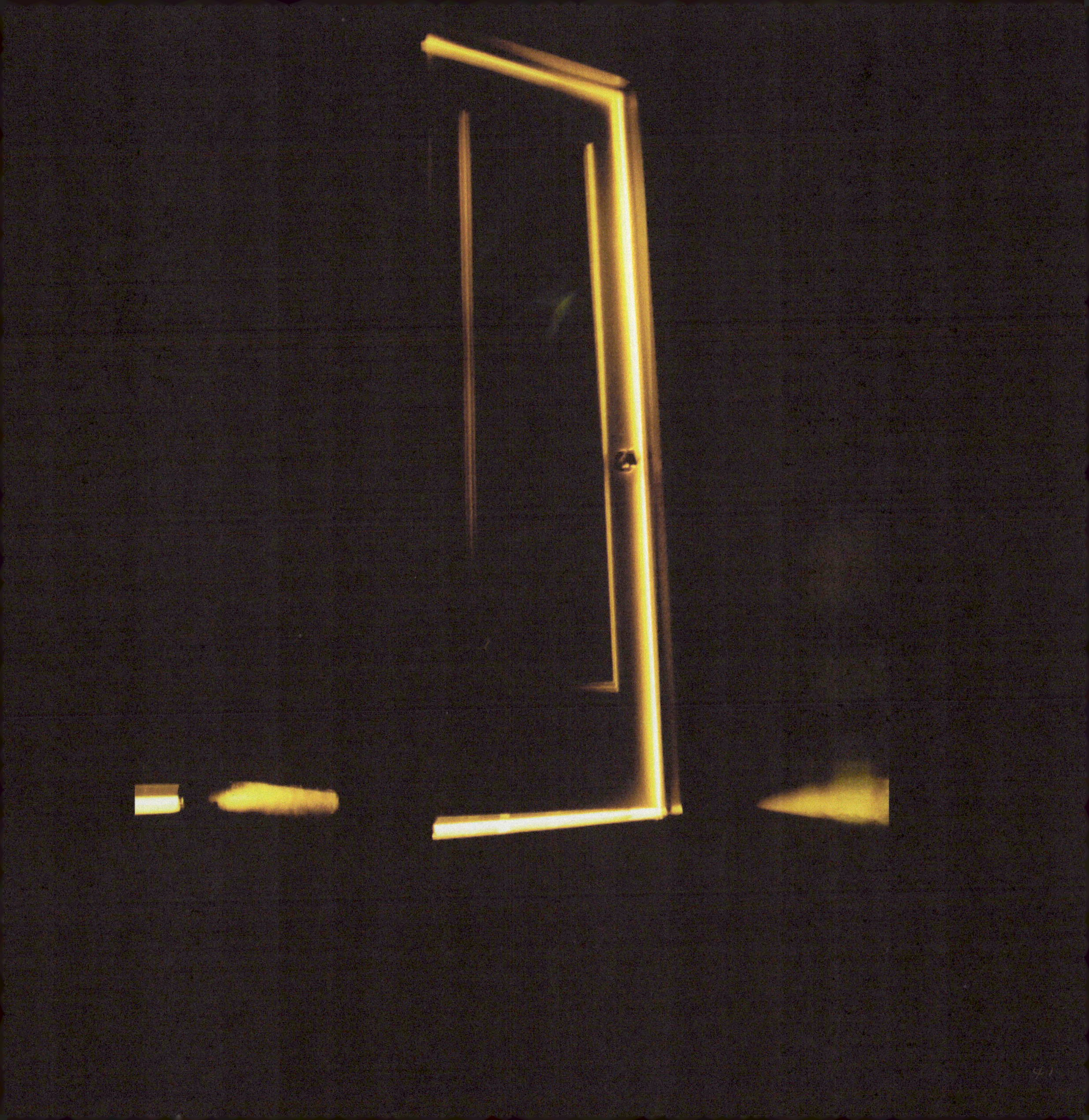

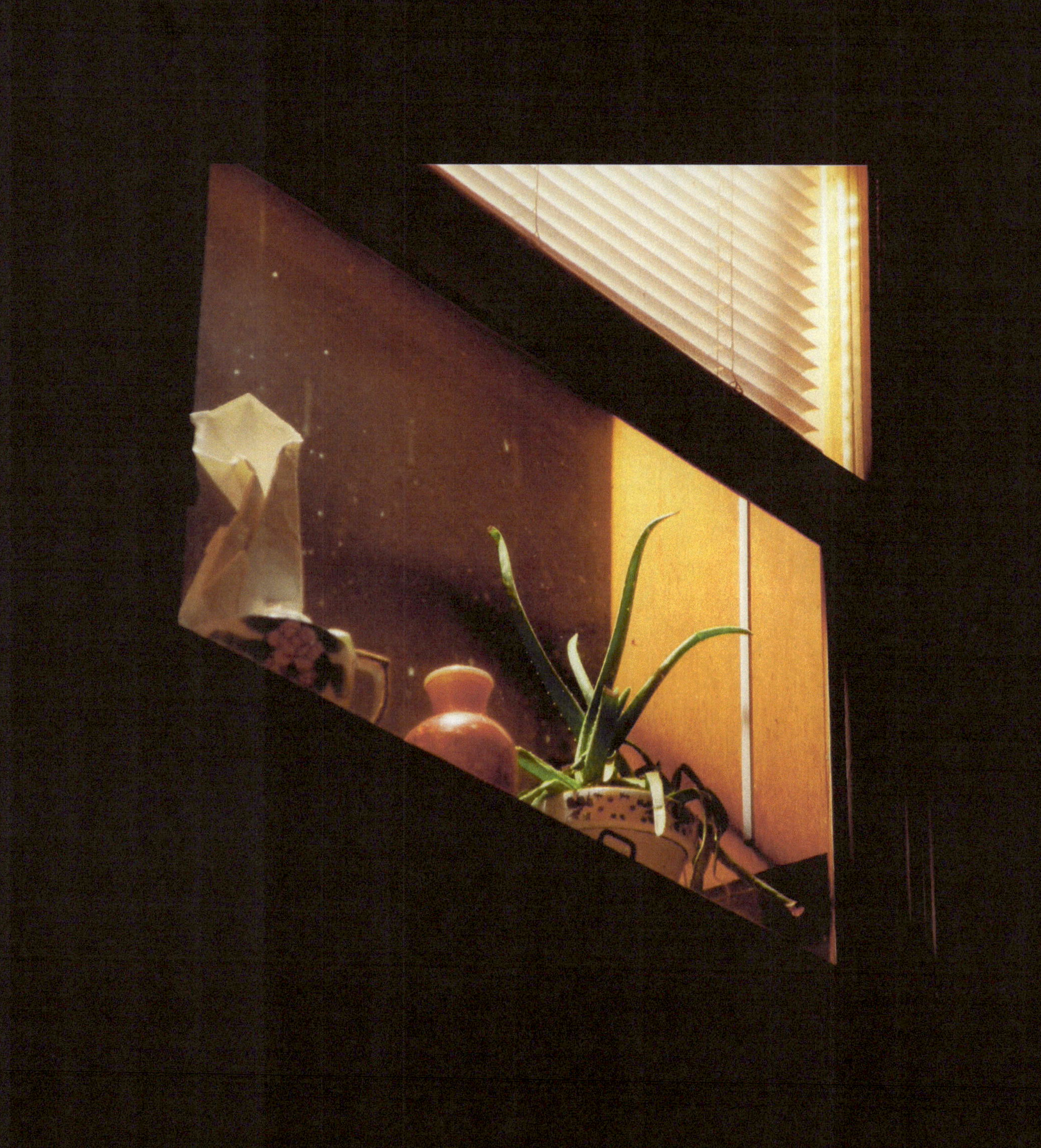

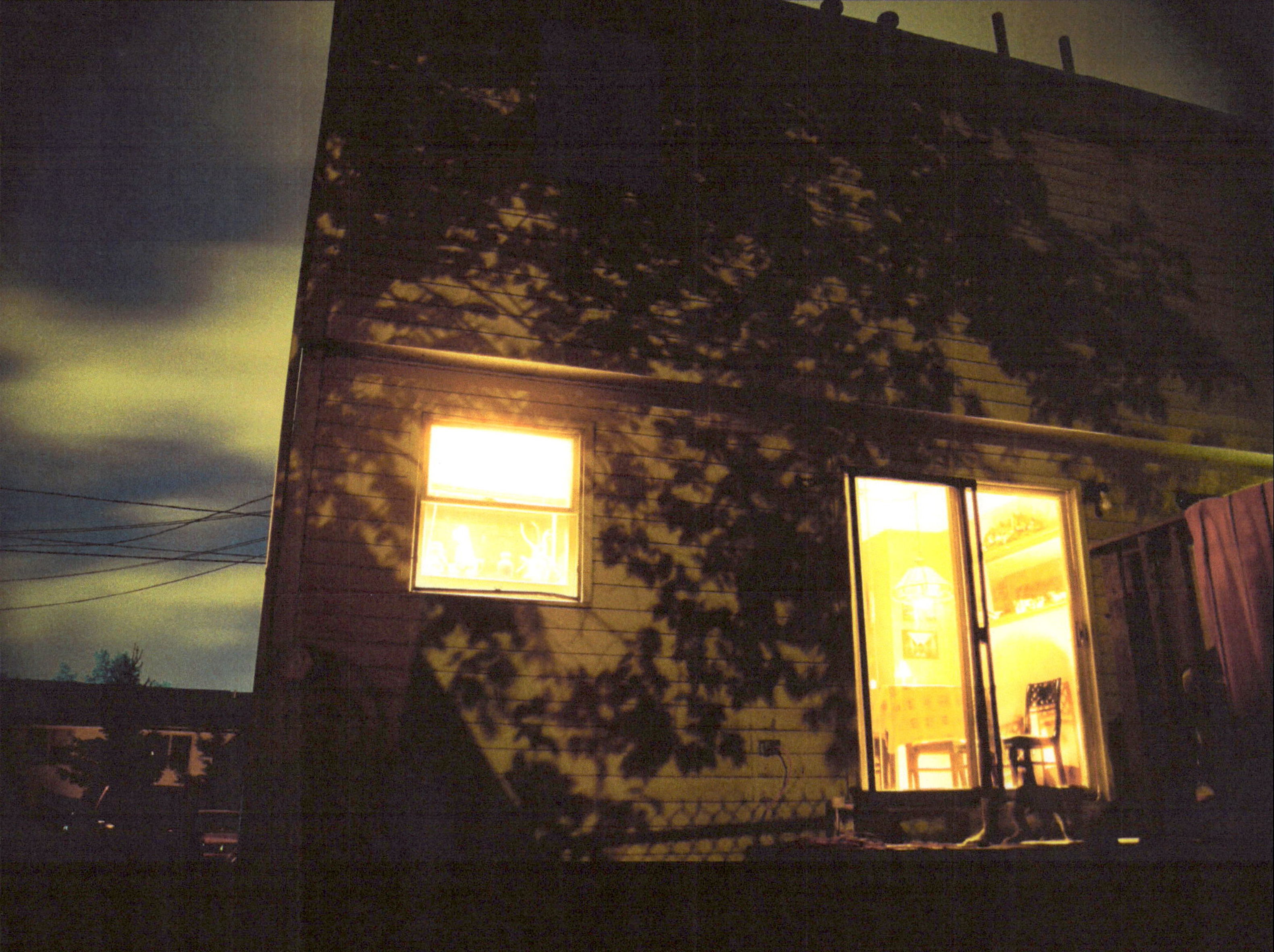

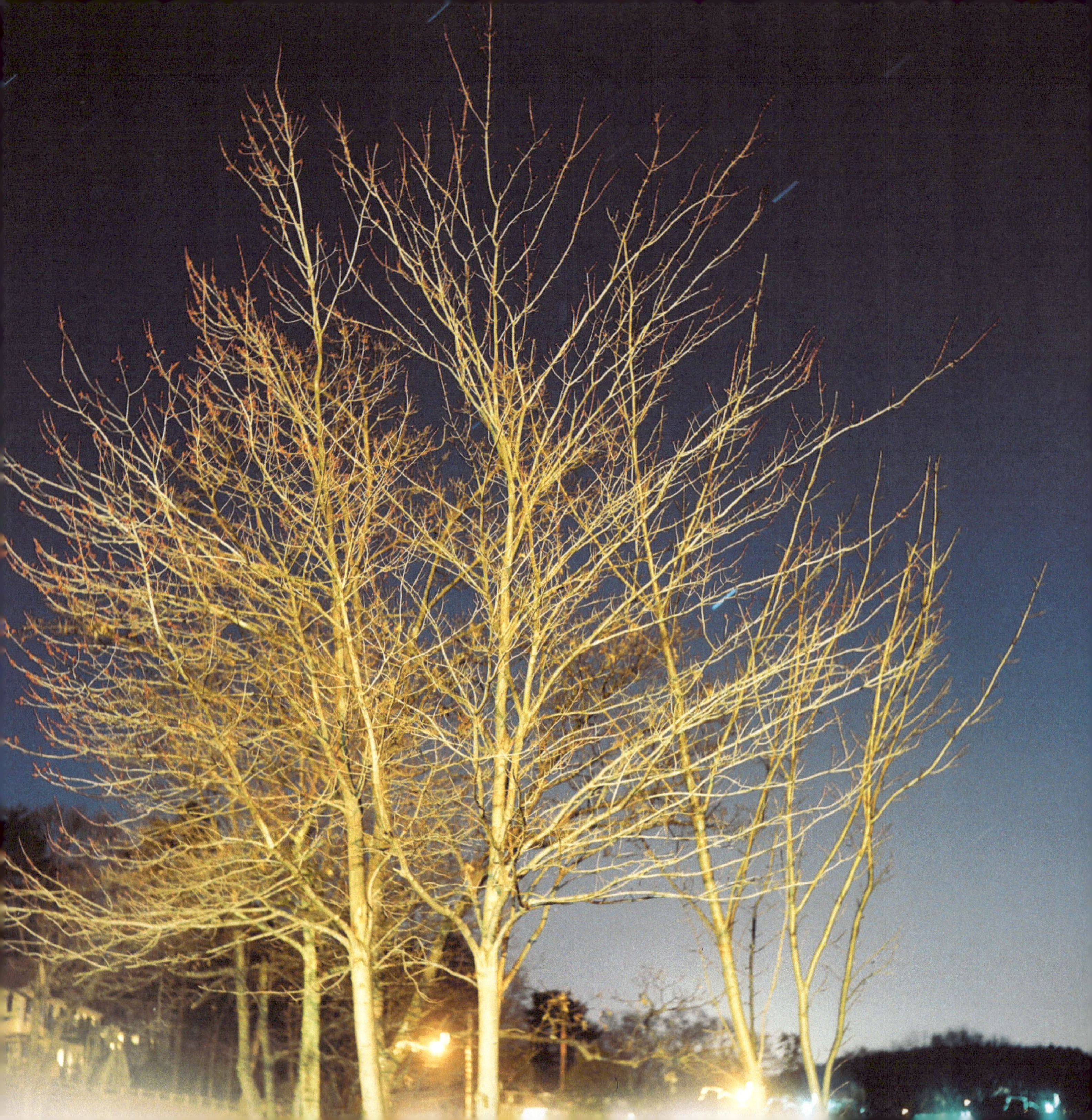

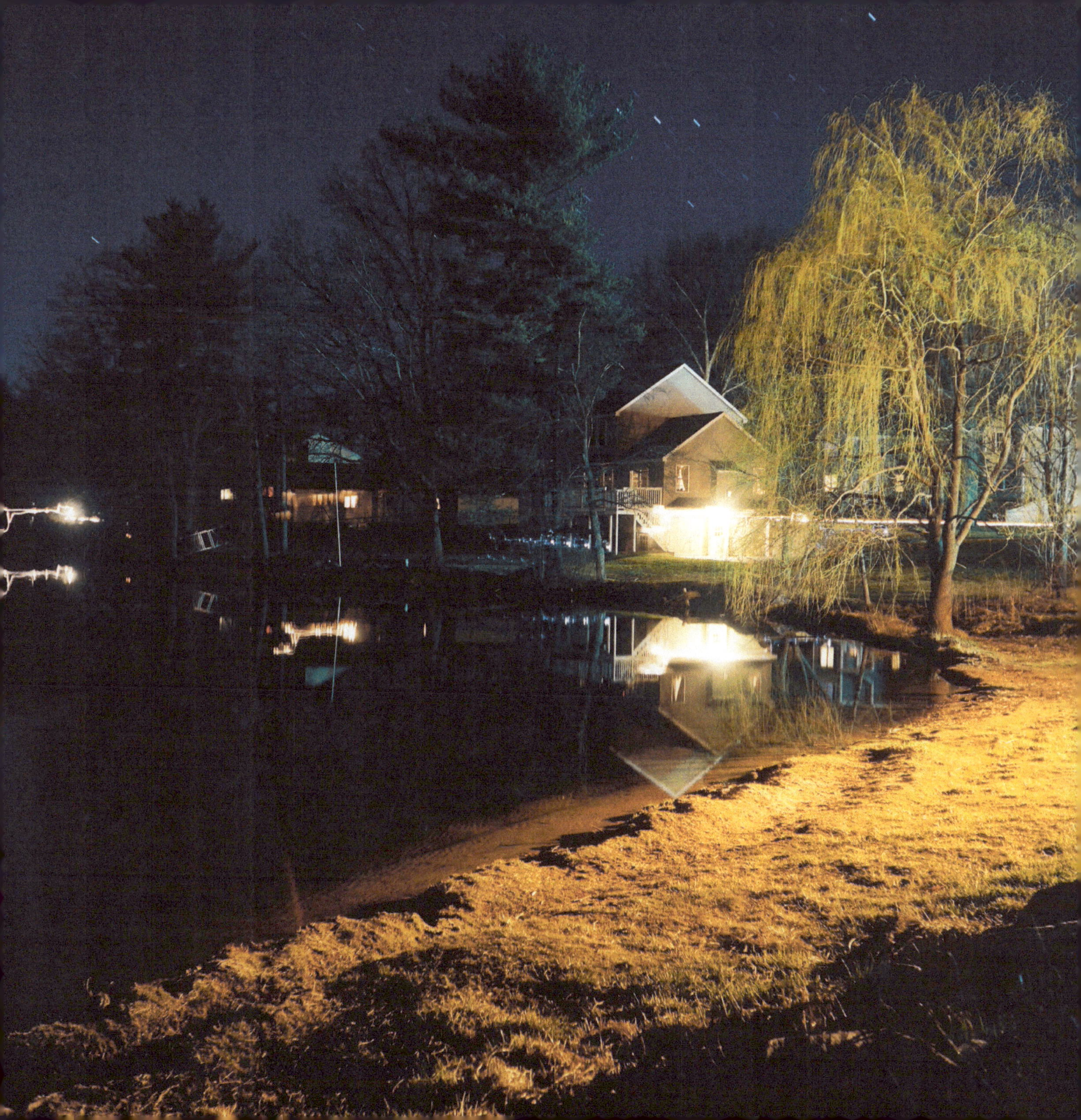

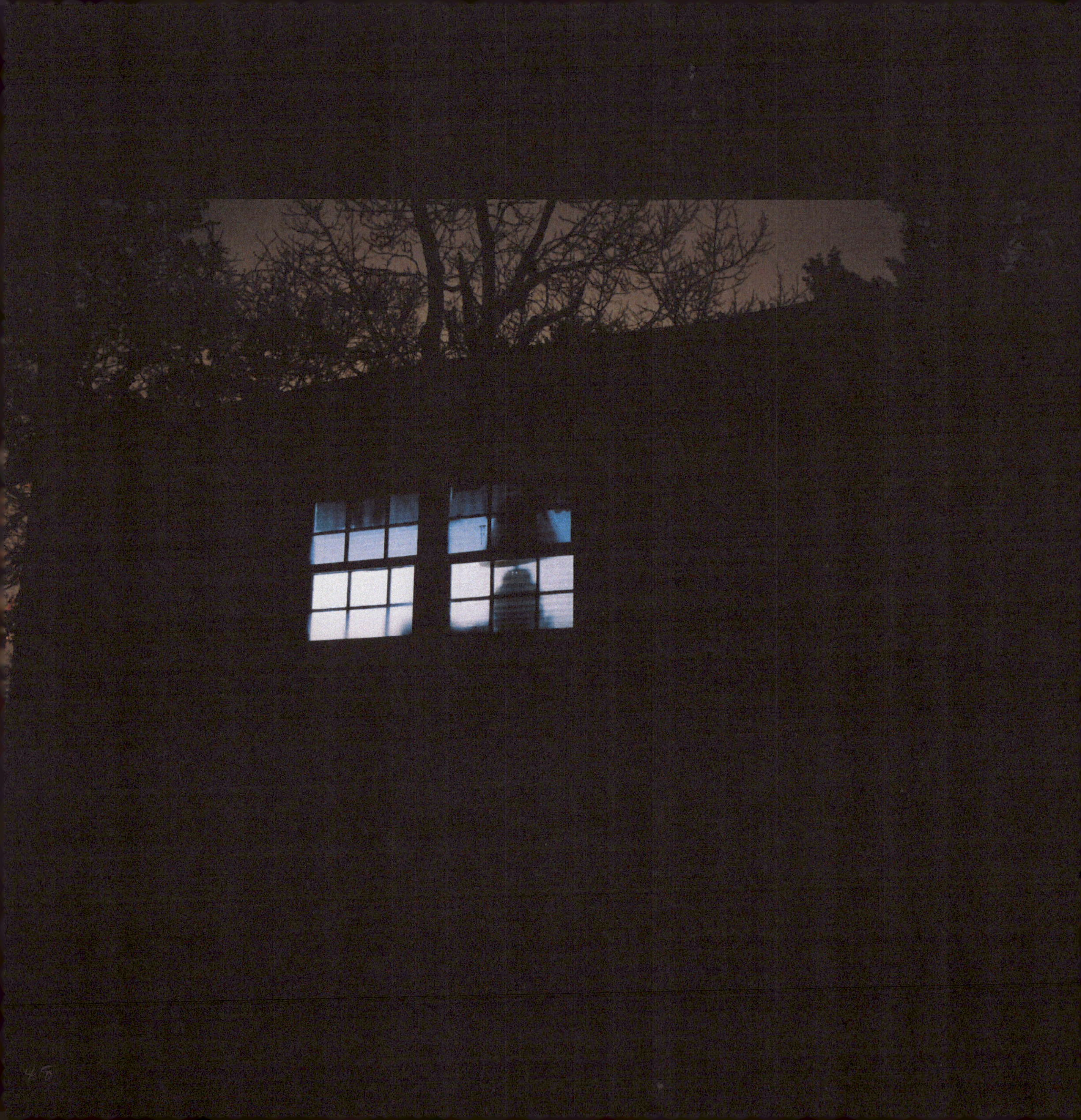

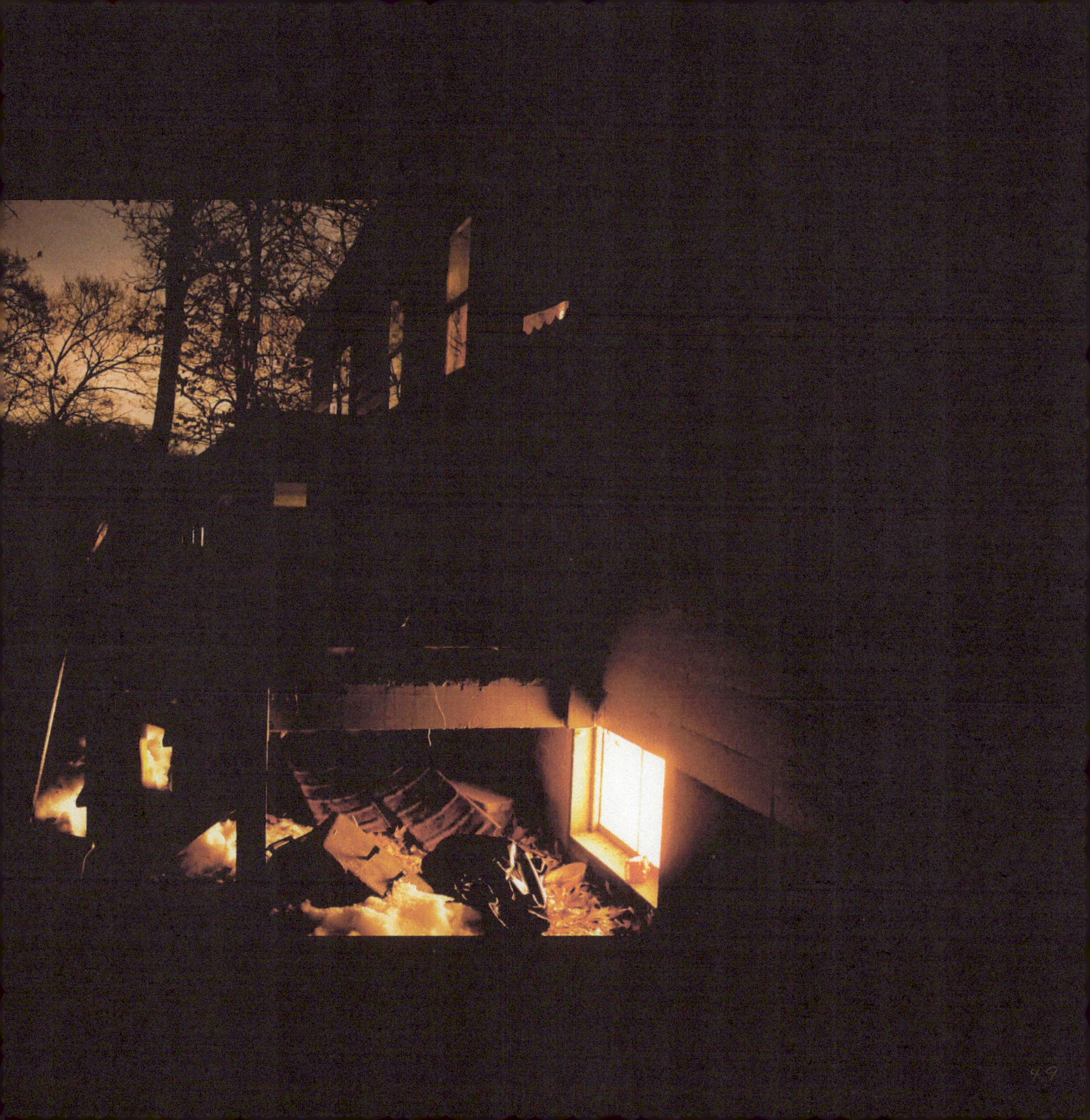

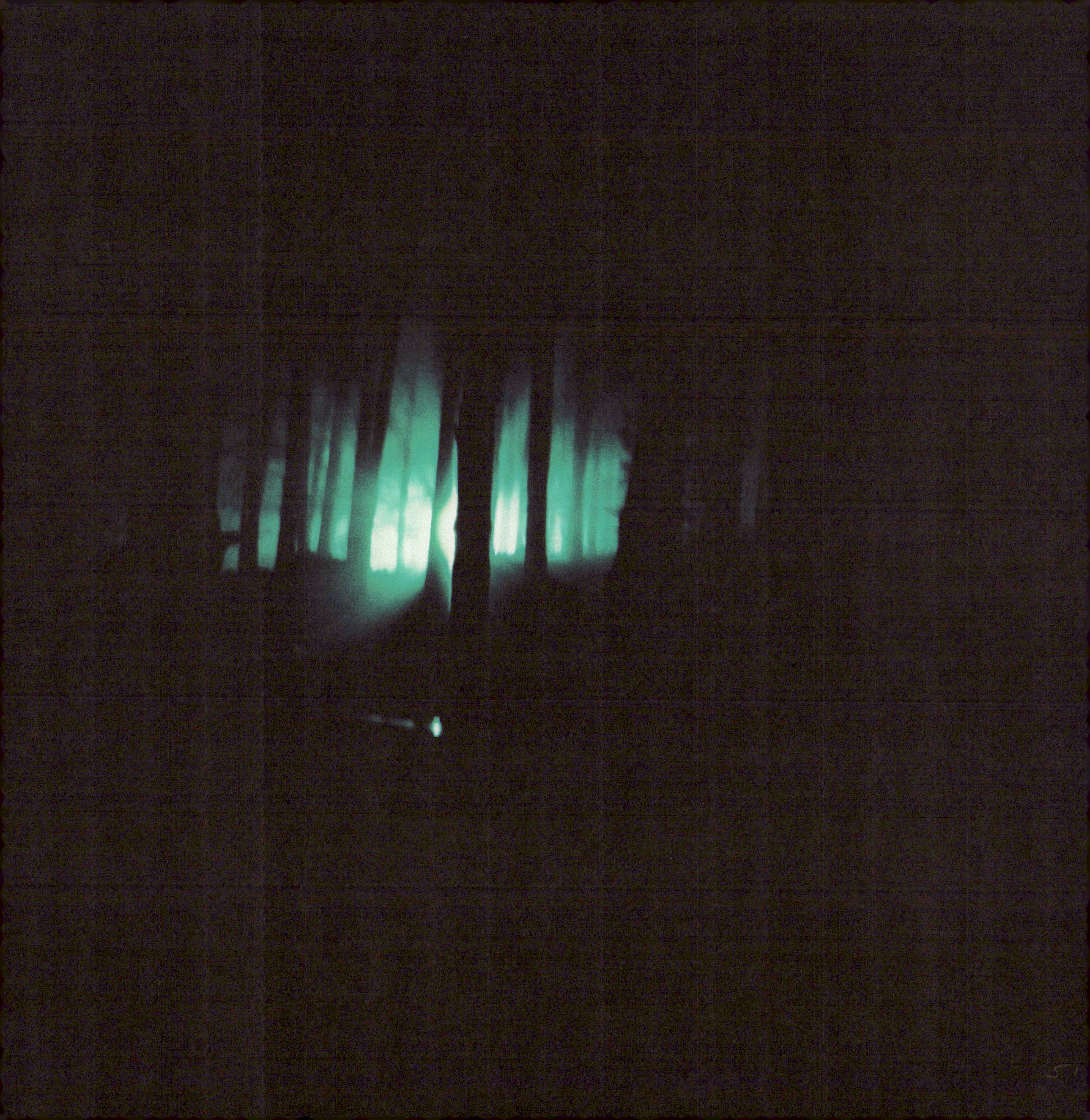

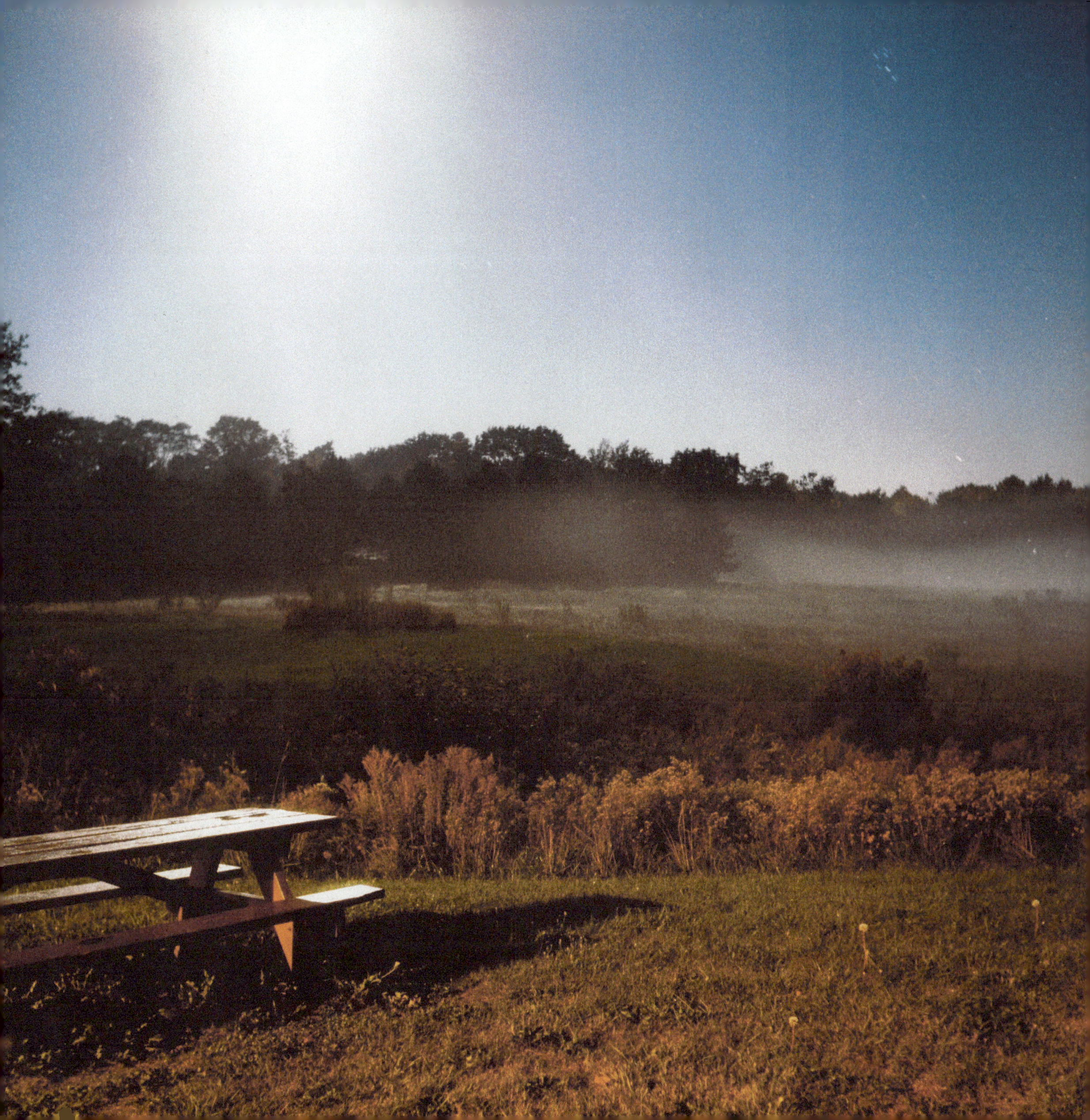

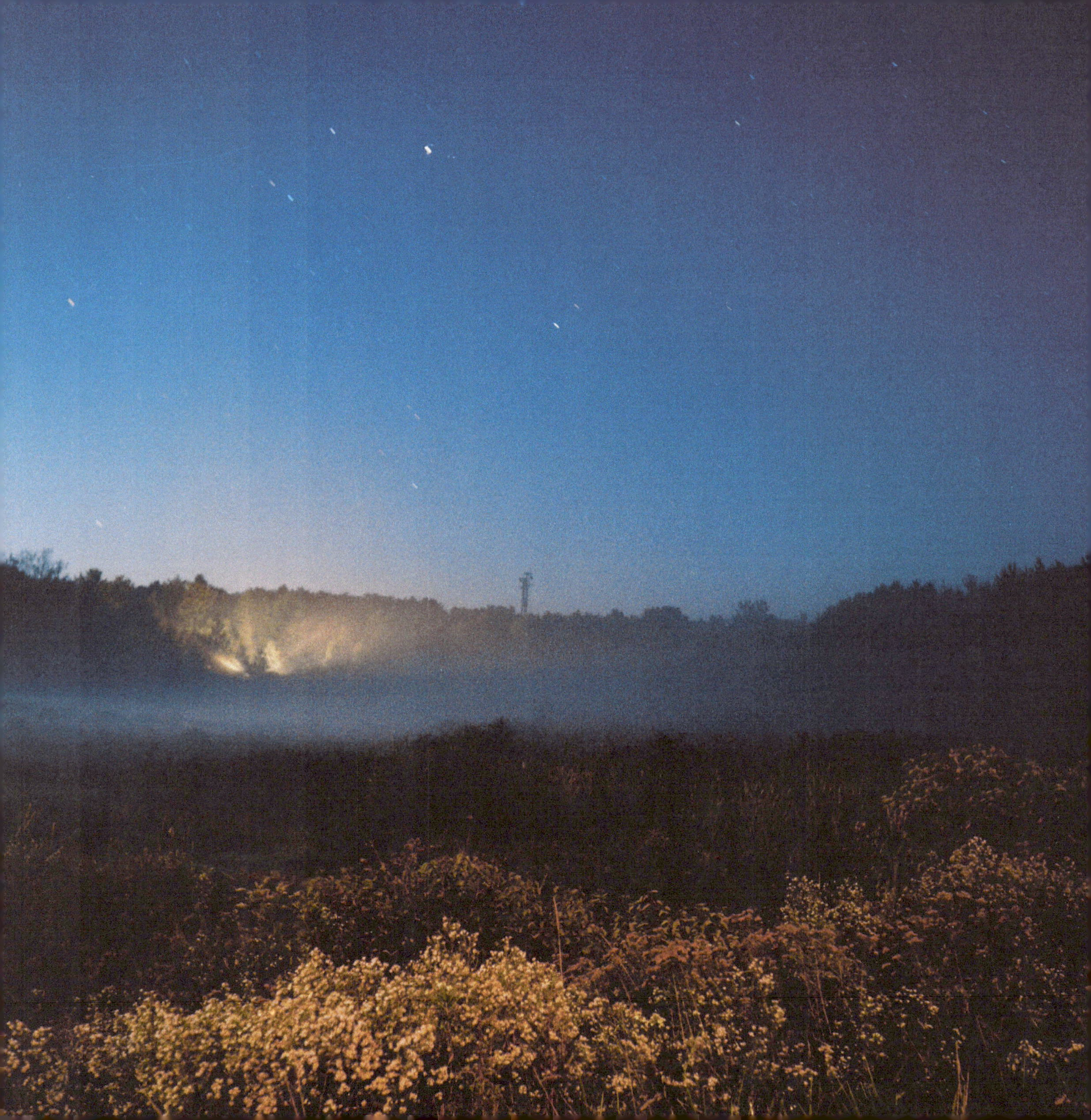

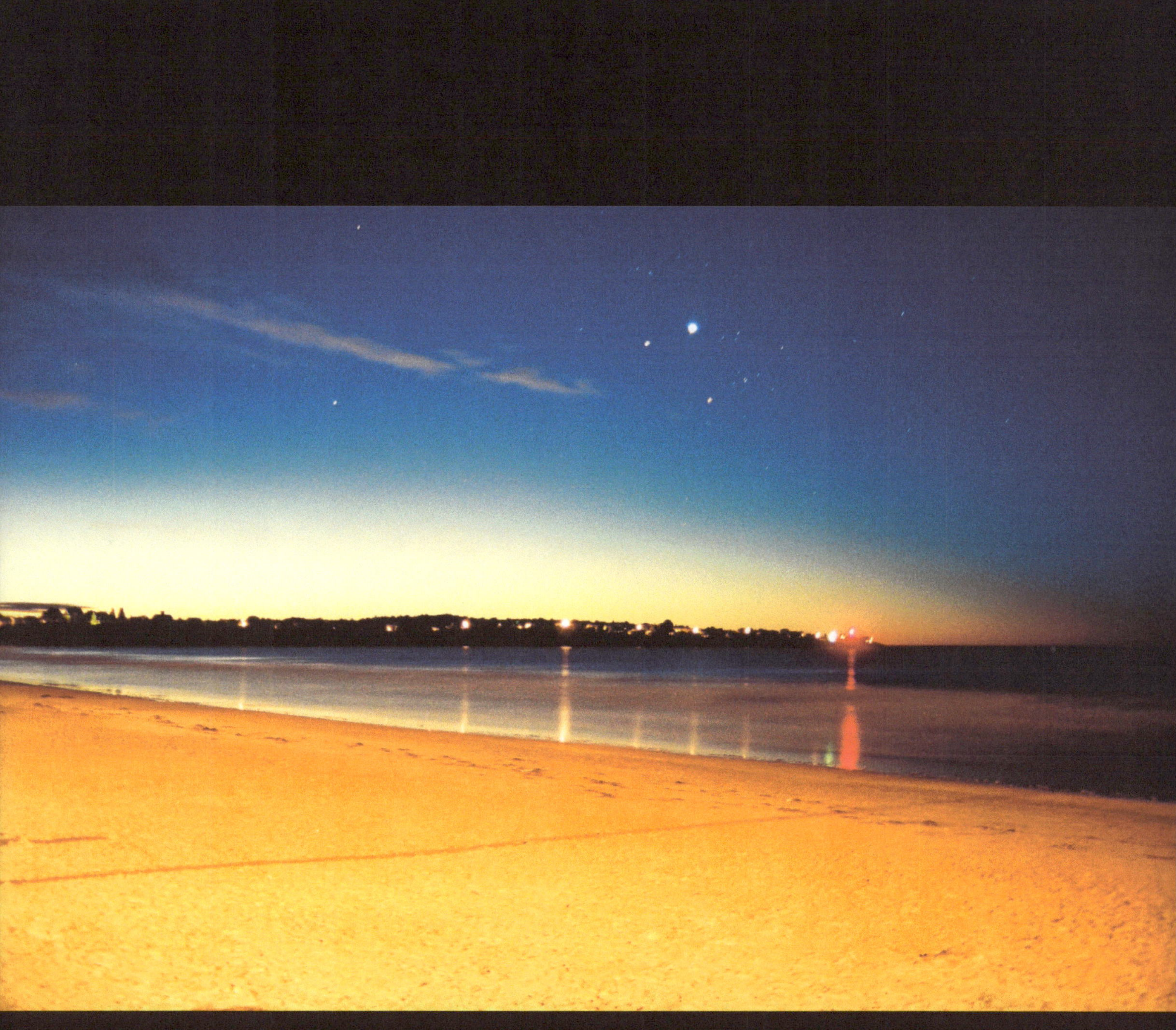

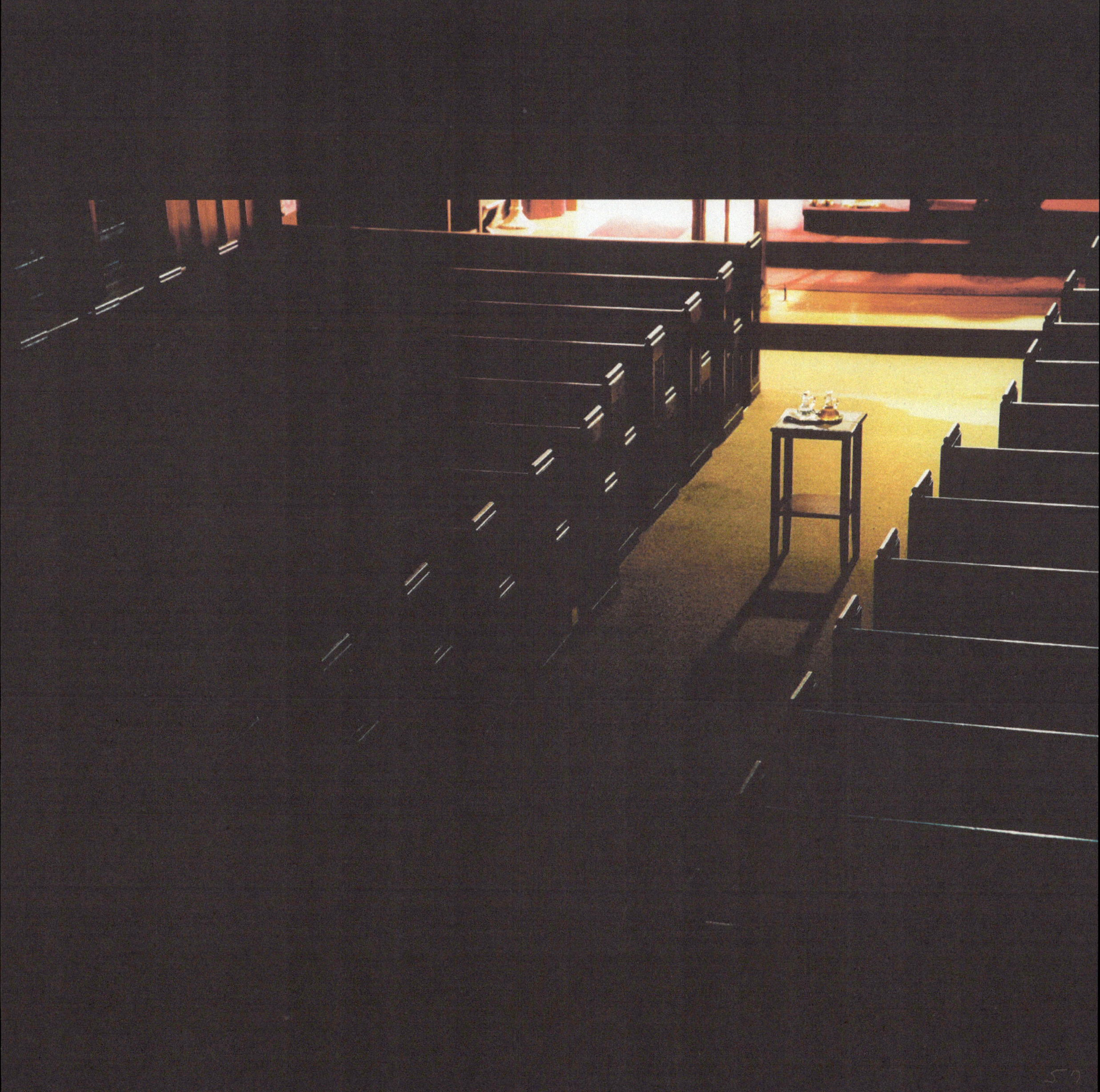

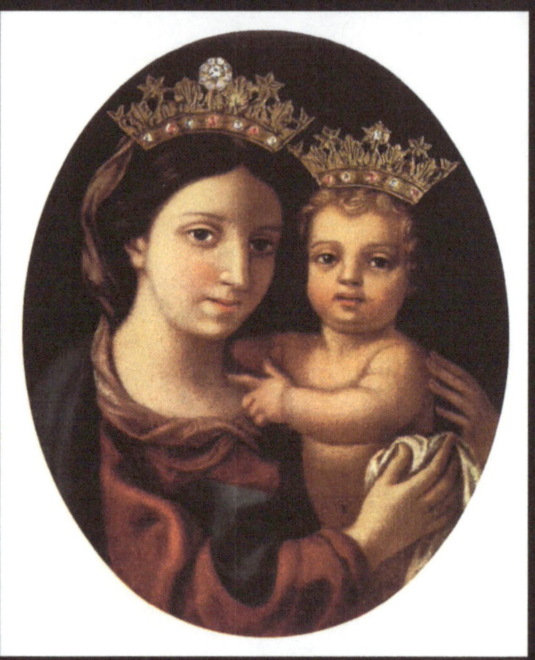

MY MOTHER, MY CONFIDENCE

UNFAILING PRAYER TO ST. ANTHONY

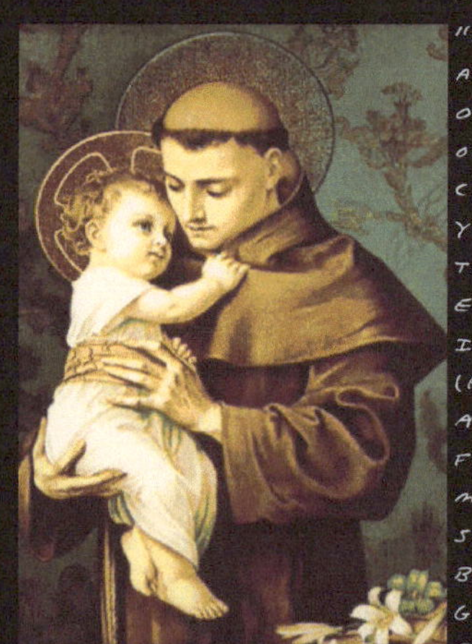

"BLESSED BE GOD IN HIS ANGELS AND IN HIS SAINTS"
O HOLY ST. ANTHONY, GENTLEST OF SAINTS, YOUR LOVE FOR GOD AND CHARITY FOR HIS CREATURES, MADE YOU WORTHY, WHEN ON EARTH, TO POSSESS MIRACULOUS POWERS. ENCOURAGED BY THIS THOUGHT, I IMPLORE YOU TO OBTAIN FOR ME (REQUEST). O GENTLE AND LOVING ST. ANTHONY, WHOSE HEART WAS EVER FULL OF HUMAN SYMPATHY, WHISPER MY PETITION INTO THE EARS OF THE SWEET INFANT JESUS, WHO LOVED TO BE FOLDED IN YOUR ARMS; AND THE GRATITUDE OF MY HEART WILL EVER BE YOURS. AMEN.

www.ingramcontent.com/pod-product-compliance
Lightning Source LLC
LaVergne TN
LVHW070145110826
845147LV00002B/330

* 9 7 8 0 6 1 5 1 6 6 7 5 9 *